DOWN EAST

LE D'ANTICOSTI
Quebec

ère aux Renards
Gaspe
Percé
Chandler
New Carlisle
DES CHALEURS

GULF OF ST. LAWRENCE

MADELEINE IS.

Tignish
PRINCE EDWARD IS.
NORTHUMBERLAND
Borden
Charlottetown
St. Peters
Souris
Georgetown

CAPE BRETON
Highlands Nat Park
Ingonish
Cabot trail
Glace Bay
Baddeck
Sydney
Bras d'Or Lake
Louisburg

hatham
ucto
Moncton
Shediac
Port Elgin
Cape Tormentine
LAND STRAIT
Aulac
Amherst
Springhill
Tatamagouche
ex
Parrsboro
MINAS BASIN
Truro
Stewiacke
Wood Is.
Caribou
Pictou
Antigonish
New Glasgow
Mulgrave

NOVA SCOTIA

Kentville
Windsor
Middleton
Bridgetown
napolis
al
Halifax

Bridgewater
Liverpool
Shelburne

ATLANTIC OCEAN

Down East

Maine, Prince Edward Island, Nova Scotia

and the Gaspé

Down East

Maine, Prince Edward Island, Nova Scotia and the Gaspé

by
SARGENT F. COLLIER

HOUGHTON MIFFLIN COMPANY, BOSTON

The Riverside Press, Cambridge

1953

Herewith this book is dedicated to the gasoline attendant, the moving spirit of any fortnightly tour on the open road. He supplieth not only the keys to the station but, in a sense, the keys to the city as well — advice, road maps, motel and hotel information, and in general offers the welcoming word — if you've got the money he's got the time. Here "Chubby" happens to be a Good Gulfer in Boston.

The Riverside Press
Cambridge • Massachusetts

Printed in the U.S.A.

PREFACE

HISTORIC ACADIA: synonymous with the region in the mind of the Maine native when he chisels the words through his nostrils, "Down East." He includes Canada — that is, its Maritimes — and as far away, possibly, as "Chaloor Bay." Acadia was used by the seventeenth-century French to designate the land of Nova Scotia, part of New Brunswick, a slice of Quebec, and eastern Maine. Our voyage will include Cape Breton Island in Nova Scotia, Prince Edward Island, and the Gaspé Peninsula.

The most accepted definition of "Down East" is that area where the prevailing southwest winds generally drove the vessels of the Yankee and Bluenose skippers down the coast. Where does "Down East" actually begin? We shall place it arbitrarily at Camden. Artistically, at least, that is where the Maine coast starts to express its character, where commerciality is left behind and the spruces thicken. Offshore, the cod is chasing the sardine and the fisherman is chasing both, and likewise trapping the lobster, monarch of them all. The water, dotted with spruce and granite islands, is icy cold, and so it will remain until the red beaches of Prince Edward Island, where some phenomenon heats up the summer bathing temperature. There will be miracles at Moncton, N.B.: a bore and a magnetic hill. Later, the tides will rise and fall to the greatest height and depth of any in the world. In the Evangeline section of Nova Scotia off Fundy bay, they sometimes reach sixty feet. At sea off Ingonish and Wedgeport, delectable giants — tuna and swordfish — will tempt amateurs with rod and reel, professionals with harpoons.

At Camden, the first spectacle is mountains meeting the sea. Lord Byron wrote of a similarly distinguished landscape in Greece, where

> The mountains look on Marathon,
> And Marathon looks on the sea —

Byron (whose grandfather, an English admiral, knew this country — he destroyed a French fleet in the Baie des Chaleurs) would have taken to our road which so often runs along the hills and the sea — at Camden, Bar Harbor, over the Cabot Trail, along the Gaspé Peninsula. Such views meant something to a young American poet of Camden, a girl of nineteen named Edna St. Vincent Millay. The first lines of "Renascence," perhaps the best poem she ever wrote, admit as much.

In 1605 a poetic little clerk named Rosier, on a ship out of England called the

Archangel, gazed at the three hills. He was recording for Captain George Waymouth, in turn exploring for Ferdinando Gorges, the man who paid the bills but never saw the area. Rosier reports that Waymouth sailed "up into the Maine" (mainland). Ergo, what more fortuitous beginning point for our chronicle — where Maine began.

This is to be the story of three bays and a river. After Penobscot Bay eventually comes Fundy (Baya Fonda, deep bay, the Portuguese called it), thence the Baie des Chaleurs (bay of heats), the south shore of the St. Lawrence, to a finis at Quebec City.

This is Champlain's country. Before him it was Cartier's. Sieur de Monts, Phips, Wolfe — this was their cruising water.

The wealthy, and he was always called "dashing," Baron de St. Castin made the rounds of Acadia too. He had served in the spit-and-polish regiment of the Carignan-Salières at Quebec to protect the populace against the Iroquois. When the regiment disbanded, St. Castin headed down the salmon rivers to the Penobscot — there had been a little trouble at cards at Quebec — to marry the beauteous daughter of an Indian chief.

Cartier, in 1534, saw the great rock of Percé when it was attached to the Gaspé Peninsula. By the time Champlain arrived it was surrounded by water. Long before the Frenchmen, came Leif Ericson — his date was A.D. 1000. His "Markland" was supposedly the Nova Scotia of today. The Cabots, John and son Sebastian, landed in 1497 on the remote eastern side of Cape Breton. It is for these Venetians, sailing in the service of England, that the dazzling Cabot Trail over the sea was named, though many proper Bostonians may believe it was otherwise.

Later several "Bostonais" did go Down East. Sir William Phips, a shepherd boy who became governor of Massachusetts and was later knighted by the king, looked in from time to time on Castine and Port Royal (Annapolis Royal, where occurred the first white settlement in the New World — Champlain's, Sieur de Monts', and Poutrincourt's doing). In fact, Phips made it all the way up to the Citadel of Quebec with an armada, where he was outsmarted and outlucked by the old French governor, Frontenac. There was a New Haven Saltonstall in trouble at the disastrous battle of Castine in 1779, where a Colonel Brewer and young Preble

Down East. Where does it begin? Some might say at the Massachusetts-New Hampshire border or where New Hampshire edges into Maine.

Others would submit that Down East starts at Wiscasset, Maine, whose old houses are as lovely as any . . .

of the American Navy fought valiantly, and General Peleg Wadsworth too, who was later captured and made good a brilliant escape. The fabulous fortress at Louisburg, which is as far Down East as we can go without getting our feet wet, was won by a prominent New England citizen, a William Pepperell, plus the aid of an English commodore named Warren who had married a colonial lady, and Governor Charles Lawrence and a Boston Winslow were undeniably hard-boiled in booting the slatternly Acadians out of Grand Pré. About ten thousand Loyalists, including hundreds of Harvard graduates, who couldn't stomach the idea of being ruled by other than a king, settled in Nova Scotia, especially at Shelburne. Some went to New Brunswick, a few to Prince Edward Island, and others even to the shores of the Gaspé Peninsula. When Evangeline and her band moved out of Acadia, Connecticut settlers moved right in.

The immortal Wolfe, the boy general, while preparing for both his Cape Breton (second Louisburg) and Quebec conquests, made Halifax his base. En route, in the Gaspesian peninsula, his men lived high on the hog of vandalism, which does not sit too well in the records. More recent exploits, other than by the sword, have brought fame — consider the inventions of such working visitors as Alexander

. . . and whose ships, too, were once beautiful. Arriving at the Boothbay area, we're almost Down East.

Graham Bell and Guglielmo Marconi on Cape Breton. On this one island alone is represented the cradle of four mediums of communication: the cable, the telephone, the radio, the airplane.

Explorers, warriors, Acadians, Loyalists, scientists, and now tourists — and Heaven be praised, as yet, not many of them, for these lands are wide and broad. In this corner of North America not all the trees lose their greenery with the passing of the season; it is always Christmas as you look at the sweep of the forests.

Neither do men lose their manners and kindliness. You'll notice *that* from the first moment you cross the border into Canada. Why are their customs officials always so much more respectful and genial than our own? Calais papers, please copy. Cartographers Cabot, Cartier, and Champlain saw what you will see, but they were born hundreds of years before L. J. M. Daguerre and Henry Ford. Today it's yours with a Brownie and a jalopy. The poor man's trip to England and France (two weeks and two hundred dollars should do it), and no passport is needed.

In closing, one hurry-up tip: See Percé Rock, while it lasts. Geologists tell us that, because of the erosion of the sea, the rock will stand for only thirteen thousand years.

It's later than you think.

THE LOG OF THE DOWN EAST TOUR

2 weeks — approximately 2000 miles

First Day. Camden to Bar Harbor — approximately 100 miles

Second Day. To motel outside St. John, New Brunswick — 210 miles

Third Day. Charlottetown, P.E.I. — 160 miles

Fourth Day. Around P.E.I. and across Northumberland Strait to Pictou (or New Glasgow, N.S.) — 150 miles

Fifth Day. To Ingonish, Cape Breton Island — 175 miles

Sixth Day. Baddeck, Cape Breton Island — 100 miles

Seventh Day. Kentville, N.S. — 200 miles

Eighth Day. Halifax or on to Lunenburg — 60 or 120 miles

Ninth Day. Digby or thereabouts — 170 miles (add 60 if from Halifax)

Tenth Day. Sidetrips: Bear River, Annapolis Royal, across Digby Ferry to Fredericton — 150 miles

Eleventh Day. Cross Maine or New Brunswick to Matapédia as it pleases — no stops, approximately 300 miles

Twelfth Day. Matapédia to Percé — 170 miles

Thirteenth Day. Percé to Metis Beach on the St. Lawrence — 250 miles

Fourteenth Day. To Quebec — 250 miles

CONTENTS

Down East begins at Camden, where the mountains first meet the sea. Shown is the Windjammer Fleet in Camden Harbor, the Camden Hills beyond. Captain Waymouth first sighted these "mountaines" when he trended into "the Maine" in 1605. Here Edna St. Vincent Millay, 300 years later, saw "three mountains and a wood."

I

Camden: Where "the Maine" Begins

FOR SOME YEARS smug motorists who know this part of Maine or who have been tipped off, and who are eager to get beyond the boundary of the Camden Hills, in fact, into the real Down East country, have turned off Route 1 sharp left just beyond Waldoboro and have crossed explorer Waymouth's Georges River at the little mill town of Warren. Thus, over a well-surfaced backwoods short cut, they have saved twenty minutes and have avoided the traffic of three coastal towns.

It sounds as if our thinking were slightly addled when we advocate eliminating Thomaston and the Knox mansion, Rockland with its great hostelry, the Farnsworth Museum, and Rubenstein's antique shop — a museum in itself — or Rockport (once part of Camden), a town full of the benefactions of the Bok family of Philadelphia, especially in music. But this is a fourteen-day, high-horsepower, mid-twentieth-century vacation for the quick and the curious. Our assignment is far beyond the tempo of 1884 when, during mud time, the stagecoach between Rockland and Rockport took seven hours to cover a distance of seven miles. Within the fleeting fortnight, we must traverse the shores of Penobscot Bay, the Bay of Fundy, Northumberland Strait, the Baie des Chaleurs, and the St. Lawrence to Quebec City, to follow by land the same routes which Cartier and Champlain pursued by sea in the sixteenth and seventeenth centuries.

1

Left: Its grace unobstructed by the presence of fall shutters, this Camden-Rockport house was once floated over the waves from Bath, Maine. Right: Cary Bok owned this house at Camden.

Left: Camden Public Library containing the old-ship-paintings collection of Parker Morse Hooper, architect of the building. Right: Lake behind Camden.

The borders of Acadia arbitrarily determine that the back route to the Camden Hills shall be our starting point by land. As for this important cutoff: a legendary sign back on the coastal Route 1 beyond Waldoboro, entitled Moose Crossing, which especially delighted alien motorists, once served as a reminder that the hard-to-find left turn was coming just above Warren.

On arriving in the bosom of Camden, we are enveloped with correctness and conservatism, and surrounded by old houses, giant elms, and white churches. Reminiscent of York Harbor, Camden is one of the more prosperous and well-kept towns in Maine and was the first village in the country to set flower boxes atop its street posts. Mary Curtis Bok Zimbalist, who gave the flower boxes, got the idea from her son Cary Bok, who first saw similar ones in England. Camden's small factories are hidden out of sight, and throughout the years it has managed to hold on to its summer population. It is here at the Smiling Cow in Camden that, for a modest sixty cents, a bargain at thrice the price, one must pick up Lew Dietz's informal, vastly interesting history of Camden and Rockport, *Camden Hills,* a book of the region, full of beautiful sketches by Carol Thayer Berry. Dietz is perhaps best known for his "Jeff White" books, a series on the Maine Woods, written for boys.

According to Dietz, André Thevet, a seagoing French priest, saw the Camden Hills in 1556 on his way north from the Kennebec. "Having left Florida," said Thevet (apparently in those days everything south of Bath was Florida), "we came upon the country of the green mountains." He was followed by Bartholomew Gosnold in search of "sassafras root, cedar and furs"; he found the coast "very pleasant to behold" and discovered to his amazement an early existence of present-day Camden summer correctness, "a pair of Christian trousers on the legs of a savage." David Ingram, a pirate trader, returned to England with tall tales about this area. "There was gold to be picked up in the streets as big as paving blocks," and, said he, "women do wear great plates of gold covering their bodies." Houses had roofs of glittering gold and silver with entrances of pure crystal. Ingram said he got tired of picking up pearls and threw them away!

2

The Frenchmen De Monts and Champlain came to investigate for themselves. In their survey of Acadia, one of their chroniclers remarked rather acidly, ". . . if this beautiful town ever existed in nature, I would like to know who pulled it down for there is nothing but houses here made of pickets and covered with bark of trees or with skins."

The name to remember, however, is Waymouth (or Weymouth), Captain George, Master of the good ship *Archangel,* in charge of an expedition sponsored by Sir Ferdinando Gorges, absentee developer of the area we know today as Maine. As was his custom, Gorges was not on board, but home in England, when the *Archangel* made landfall in 1605 off Cape Cod. Plans to sail south were upset by contrary winds, which as usual blow toward the east — "Down East," and the *Archangel* soon found itself off the "Great Mountains."

3

Aristocrat of about 1845 with widow's walk topside. Belfast, "broiler capital" of Maine, is the home of the Belfast & Moosehead Lake Railroad, a thirty-three-mile-track cracker-barrel railroad system owned by its townspeople.

The quoted words are from the journal of Waymouth's erudite little clerk, James Rosier, for whom Cape Rosier, opposite Castine, was named. He goes on to say: "Tuesday, 11 of June, we passed up into the river with our ship, about six and twenty miles . . . the river itself, as it runneth up into the Maine . . . towards the great mountains. . . . Ten of us with our shot, and some armed, with a boy to carry powder and match, marched up . . . about four miles in the Maine, and passed over three hills."

"Runneth up into the Maine" was, incidentally, the first usage of the term Maine in this hemisphere from which the state subsequently derived its name. According to the genial Camden sage, John Whiting Webber, it may have been that Gorges chose the name for that part of France called Maine whose rulers were not only his kin but also were connected with his English queen. And the river of which Rosier speaks was the St. George, today the narrow Georges, which empties into the sea at Thomaston, and the "great mountains" the Camden Hills.

So many of the dramatis personae of America's East Coast history duplicated the format of their explorer predecessors. Columbus, to prove his arrival in a new land, brought back San Salvador savages to the court of Ferdinand and Isabella. Jacques Cartier shanghaied poor trusting Donnacona and his tribesmen for a one-way trip to France. Waymouth was the first Maine coast tourist to bring back souvenirs, and live ones at that. The Indian women off Camden were smart. They kept out of sight. But the curiosity of the braves, when trinkets were dangled, was too much. Five of the Indians were lured on board the *Archangel* for a free trip to England, to be ogled in the streets of London.

One hundred and fifty years elapsed before settlers came to the Camden Hills. Previously John Smith looked in during an extremely bad winter, pronounced the country "something to affright rather than delight." In 1692 the Council of Plyouth granted land from the Muscongus to the Penobscot to John Beauchamp and Thomas Leverett. Beauchamp died, and Leverett, happy and successful in Boston, forgot about Camden. Later, his grandson, President of Harvard, found the title so confused that he divided the claim into shares from which Twenty Associates were formed. It was from this twenty, Dietz tells us, that Camden was established. The land was to include Appleton, Hope, Montville, Camden, and Rockport. The name — Cambden, as originally spelled — was used as early as 1768. It may be but coincidence that Lord Cambden had been an ardent friend of the colonists before the Revolution.

Left: Again the widow's walk — Searsmont. Right: Lodging for the night, Lincolnville (where one may take the ferry to Islesboro).

One of the very early Belfast architectural triumphs sporting Ionic pillars. It was regarded then just as much out of the question to raise a frame without rum (for "mechanical purposes") as it was to go through haying time without rain. As for a certain rum punch, half a dozen pail fulls would raise a dwelling house, ell, or barn, but as late as 1818 two barrel fulls were required to raise the Unitarian meetinghouse.

"The green mountains" which brought "affright" to John Smith scared not a smidgen young James Richards, who came with his family in 1768. In fact, little did. There is a firm legend that Richards rode a youngish bear down the slopes of Mount Battie when out hunting with another stem winder, friend Leonard Metcalf. Throughout the wild descent Richards tried to cut the animal's throat with a knife that kept closing in his hand. At the bottom, however, there was Metcalf to dispatch his pal's odd mount with a hatchet blow. Richards, during his Camden days, was supposed to have accounted for at least seventy moose and thirty bear, the forepaw of one of the latter big enough to fill "a peck measure." Richards' cabin was built under Mount Battie, land that passed on to his heirs for over a hundred years. That his wife Betty gave her name to the mountain has been disputed. The area of Negunticook, now called Megunticook, was as wild as it was beautiful. Occasionally, says Dietz, a few Indians came to Betty's dooryard and would sharpen their knives, but she learned to forget about her uneasiness.

With the arrival of the Richards family, Camden was on its way. Henceforth it would have its share of the virile and the spectacular.

Once, during the Revolution, an English barge, or "shavingmill," which the

5

Perry's Nut House, Belfast. Guava jellies, bits and bites from the tropics all the way to Penobscot Bay. Right: Something quite different in Belfast architecture.

Tories operated so exasperatingly, came ashore; its occupants sacked the house and slaughtered the livestock of Robert Jameson, a particularly outspoken rebel. Jameson, however, had the memory and strength of an elephant. After the war he met up with one of the shavingmill traitors, crashed a fist to his jaw, and tossed another American quisling into a roaring fireplace. Leonard Metcalf tried a daring stunt when a British schooner made into a cove. He drilled imaginary troops at the top of his voice while Andrew Wells beat a snare drum behind a bush. Metcalf, Wells, William Gregory, and Peter Ott were enlisted in Saltonstall's fiasco attempt to dislodge the British at Castine.

After Castine, the British were in command of the Camden area for a lengthy period. Raiders knocked out the bung from a keg of rum at Peter Ott's tavern. Elizabeth, the innkeeper's daughter, came shouting, "Stop, you villains." The amazed invaders retired in confusion while she held her hand over the spurting liquid. Elizabeth was courted and won by John Harkness, a young lieutenant whose boldness must have received her approval. British marauders once had ransacked his hut and stolen his musket. Harkness silently followed their trail, snatched his piece from their campfire, and, pointing it at their heads, backed off into the forest.

Later, Camden's first town meeting was held at Peter Ott's tavern. Ott was also first keeper of the town pound. Peter Ott's own son favored the English spelling of the family name, Oat. Father and son died within a year of each other and are buried side by side under a single headstone marked Ott-Oat.

Early Camdenites were responsible for the celebrated shape of the doughnut, or at least for the hole. One of the first settlers was William Gregory, whose grandson, Hanson Crockett Gregory, as a young boy sampling his mother's fry cakes suggested that she cut out the doughy centers. Forthwith the dunker's delight had been created. A cup of coffee had a companion for life.

When news of the victory in the Revolution came to Camden, revelers gathered at Robert Thorndike's. After bread, cheese, and fish, the "occaba" was passed around and they drank "to the health of the prominent actors in the struggle . . . marched around the hogshead, drinking of its contents, and growing more merry under its influence. . . . The festivities were kept up until morning."

6

Historian Locke felt a local obligation to editorialize, "The actions of men are to be judged in the light of influence with which they are surrounded and hence no further apologies are here required for the way our patriot settlers gave vent to the ebullition of their feelings at the success of their country's cause."

Camden, a most temperate town on the coast today, was to have another bout with drinking after 1812, when poor crops and general postwar depression followed. In 1817 the town warrant prescribed "to see what measures the town will adopt for the purpose of preventing retailers within the town of Camden selling spiritous liquor to be drunk." The Camden temperance society was organized, its members resolving not to drink spiritous liquors "unless they deemed it necessary." Joseph Stetson, shipbuilder who launched more than seventy vessels from Camden ways, was to be known as the "Deacon" — he had changed the crew's rations from rum to coffee.

In the "Sailor's War" (the War of 1812), the Maine coast was infested with enemy craft. Nonetheless, Camden, like all upper Maine coast towns, was engaged in blockade running or privateering. A set of sails stripped from a vessel just before the War of 1812 which violated the embargo act were found hidden years later in the cellar of the old William Carleton house on Camden Street.

When in 1812 Castine, across the bay, fell a second time to the British, Camden expected an attack momentarily. Two twelve-pounders sent from Boston were dragged up Mount Battie by ox teams. Camden was an armed camp by the time the British fleet appeared in the bay.

The British, however, just sailed past. A few landed in nearby Northport and used some outrageous language to a Mrs. Crowell, ripped open her beds, and tossed the feathers to the winds. This was the same year that the British privateer with the glorious name *Thinks I to Myself* landed troops at Clam Cove; but they were dispersed by a group of embattled farmers. The village expected serious business, however, when its Noah Miller, a patriot-pirate, sailing with armed crew in a reach boat, took a British merchantman. Sure enough, a few days later a warning flag raised from the top of Mount Battie announced an unwelcome visitor. The *Furieuse,* bristling with armament, had dropped her hook off The Ledges; her officers made threats to put Camden and Lincolnville to the torch unless the ship and cargo plus $80,000 be produced almost immediately. As Dietz records, the town no longer had the cargo, and certainly didn't have the money. While two negotiators stalled for time, Camden manpower was mustered. Then, for no particular reason, the British frigate set sail; the two Camden hostages they had taken were released at Castine.

Already the guard atop Battie had relaxed. According to a squib in John Whiting Webber's charming essay, "The High Mountains of Penobscot," a captain and staff, checking up one night, climbed the mountain and found only one man at his post, and he was fast asleep. "All of his comrades had gone to a husking party."

Perhaps both the mountain watchers and the *Furieuse* had received advance intelligence of an impending surrender, for shortly news of peace burst upon Camden. According to Dietz, "the town was aroused this cold February night by the wild clatter of hooves on the icy road and the hooting of the stage horn. At dawn the next morning, a roaring crowd scaled Mount Battie, led by Simeon Tyler, and the guardian cannon on the summit signalled victory to the countryside."

Camden now beat swords back into plowshares and had time to consider the

Smelting activity on the Penobscot River near Winterport.

improvement of the soul and intellect. Before the turn of the century, the Commonwealth had slapped Camden with a fine of two pounds, fourteen shillings, and one sixpence for being too slow at organizing a church, and for failing to support a minister. Camden then engaged a series of itinerate preachers, and pews were auctioned with individual subscriptions ranging from fifteen to three hundred and fifteen dollars. One last will and testament acknowledges conveying "one undivided half of a pew."

In 1815 Camden officially called its first minister. His salary was pegged at $500 per annum plus a third of a lot on Goose River. In the year of the preacher's coming John Norton, up the coast in the next town of Lincolnville, "made an unnatural fool of himself" by imbibing to excess and "swallowed a piece of unmasti-

A net spread for drying always makes a subject for the photographer.

cated meat and choked to death." Over in Camden, however, sights were up, for about this time a literary society was formed, and Dietz reports that in one of their first debates it was argued: "Is it probable that the American republic will be in Existence at the End of the Nineteenth Century? A Mr. Codman assumed the affirmative. A Mr. Storer and a Mr. Talbot took a dim view of the issue."

For many years, even before Maine had broken away from Massachusetts in 1820 to become the twenty-third state, Camden had been working out a constructive shipbuilding existence, and today she still launches the best. Prior to the Civil War, over a hundred vessels carried Camden in solid letters beneath their taffrails.

Eventually Camden was to hear the portents of its third war. On a fall day in the sixties, a steamboat carrying the Little Giant, Stephen Douglas, called at Camden harbor, and it is reported that Camden turned out to a man, cheering him to the echo. Yet a few weeks later Camden went to the polls and, with true Maine immutability, voted Republican, and overwhelmingly in favor of Abe Lincoln.

Camden's immortal hero of the Civil War was a glorious old salt named William Conway who had spent three-quarters of his sixty years in the American Navy. Stationed at Pensacola in Florida, when a rebel force appeared he was ordered by his superiors to strike the flag. "I won't do it, sir," the old man replied. "That's the flag of my country." The legend on a several-ton boulder, pulled from the back country by four span of horses, proves that on August 10, 1906, "Conway Day," the town got around to honoring him.

After the Civil War, when Holly Bean took over, Camden achieved its greatest prominence as a shipbuilding town. The place was chockablock full of ship car-

The celebrated Bucksport Grave with its three-way legend. One version: Judge Buck's jealous wife dictated that her husband condemn their housekeeper as a witch. As promised at gallows the victim haunted him forever, since the outline of her leg appeared indelibly on the Judge's gravestone.

penters, chandlers, sailmakers, sparmakers, figure-head carvers, and riggers. Over on the Rockport shore in 1885 the *Frederick Billings* slid down the ways, the largest square-rigger ever water-borne on the shores of Penobscot Bay. Seven years later the *Billings* was in bad luck off Chile and sank in twenty minutes.

It was of interest to Dietz that during this era both the Camden and Rockport settlements "had a finger in lime." But with the coming of new kilns, which took less time, burned faster, and did not require the fires drawn after each processing, the old-time operator had to throw in the sponge. The "limers" themselves had to be sound. If a fire broke out on a leaky vessel, there wasn't much you could do but seal the vessel tighter, plaster every crack, and pray that the blaze would smother. Water was lime's deadliest enemy.

When war came in 1917, Camden went back to building ships. "During the Second World War," Dietz continues, "the Bean Yard was the Camden Shipbuilding and Marine Railway Company and in the hands of three newcomers, Richard Lyman, Clinton Lunt and Cary Bok, son of one of the region's greatest benefactors, Mary Louise Bok (later Mrs. Efrem Zimbalist). This time when the call came for ships it was all but too late. Those men who had known the trade were gone or too old to work proficiently. A few old timers remained, but it was younger men who filled the ranks. They came from stores, garages, farms or business — fifteen hundred of them at the peak of construction. Learning came astonishingly easy for it was in their blood."

In the field of artistic creation, Camden has produced one of our greatest poets. In this respect the old Hathaway house on Chestnut Street is important. Its original owner, John Hathaway, Camden's first lawyer, soon after arriving in town in 1796 "took sick" and died of typhus. Memories were not sufficient, however, to prevent his wife, Deborah Cushing, from enjoying the house until her death at ninety-one. Here Edna St. Vincent Millay, called Vincent in Camden, one of the most articulate poets of her generation (born in Rockland eight miles away on Washington's Birthday in 1892), grew up with her mother and two sisters. She was graduated from Vassar in 1917; in later years she married Eugen Boissevain, and the pair lived on the poetess's two-acre island, Ragged Island, off South Harpswell. Her volume of poems, *The Ballad of the Harp-Weaver,* in 1923 won the Pulitzer Prize. Then there were *The Buck in the Snow, Wine from These Grapes, Huntsman, What Quarry?* and other collected verses, an output very possibly nurtured in the beginning by the Camden scene, such sweep of vision as poets, artists, philosophers require from the coast of Maine.

It would seem that in "Renascence" she was paying early tribute to the three Camden Hills — and the sea beyond — "the things that bounded":

> All I could see from where I stood
> Was three long mountains and a wood;
> I turned and looked another way,
> And saw three islands in a bay.
> So with my eyes I traced the line
> Of the horizon, thin and fine,
> Straight around till I was come
> Back to where I'd started from;
> And all I saw from where I stood
> Was three long mountains and a wood.
>
> Over these things I could not see:
> These were the things that bounded me.

The Mother Church at Castine, another Maine example of the Bulfinch belfry
and Paul Revere bell, for years gathering place of the annual and special meetings
of the town of Castine, noted for its simple lines, finely arched windows and
pilastered facade. Its walls listened to a eulogy on the death of Washington,
heard fiery debate against the federal government at the time of the embargo
and nonimportation acts, which were ruining the business of Maritime Castine.
The town's sailors and soldiers have worshiped here before going off to war.
It has seen court trials and happy bridals, and has looked on the last rites of
honored and beloved citizens. It is still a place of worship.

II

Castine: Town History for the Tabloids

AFTER BUCKSPORT, skip down one hill and up another. A backward glance and that's Orland before leaving the road by a right turn for a fourteen-mile ride eastward to the peninsula of Castine.

Nearing the objective, a sign suggests either way. It makes no difference which, for Castine is on a dead end. Not dead perhaps, but sleeping. Large and small historical signs everywhere proclaim that Castine's remote past was anything but inactive; in fact, it was the battle line of five nations (French, English, Dutch, and American, not forgetting the Indians).

Each fall the billboards and their weathered calligraphy are taken down and brought forth again in the spring. One sign indicated particular goings-on in Indian times: "Upon these heights in 1692 James Giles, a boy and an Englishman taken at Casco, held in Slavery by Madockawano for attempting to escape, were tortured by fire, compelled to eat their noses and ears and then burned to death at the stake."

The old hilltop golf course was once honeycombed with the rifle pits of Revolutionary soldiers. An errant golf ball may come to rest among the grassy ramparts or in the moated ditch of old Fort George, or skirt the ovens built by the Dutch when they captured the fortifications in 1674.

Thirty-eight miles from the nearest railroad, Castine hasn't been much in the national news except in 1952 when a bear was discovered across the harbor on wooded Cape Rosier, breaking a hundred-year boast that there were no bruins in the area. That same summer, the showers, for some unknown reason, by-passed Castine, and tired drinking water had to be transported by Navy ships from Bucksport and Bar Harbor. Meanwhile, the town fathers drank soda pop and searched for leaks in the age-old water system. Historians suggested that the two earthquakes that Castine experienced in 1760 and 1820 had, after all these years, upset the equilibrium of the springs.

Although the town from 1612 to 1812 was constantly under arms, it later became famous for its shipbuilding and lumber trade. It still retains some of its graceful old houses, fan windows, flying staircases. A structure pulled down a few years ago revealed massive three-inch pine planks, the seams calked like a ship. Castine, on a direct line between Nova Scotia and Boston, with its inviting harbor tucked just below the lower jaw of the wide Penobscot, beckoned to all the mariners of Acadia. Then the decline of shipping put the area out on a limb.

In the middle of the past century, Castine imported salt in her own ships from

Midshipman on postman duty at Maine Maritime Academy plods up the hill past typical Castine architectural gem.

Spain and England and stored it in vast salt-houses. At one time five hundred vessels were counted in the harbor. Castine has a greater depth of water than any other nearby port and offers sufficient fathoms for the training ships of the Maine Maritime Academy, whose buildings are on the hill above town.

In the year 1604, a date important in the foundation of all Acadia, Champlain named Mount Desert Island, and likewise the French cartographer-mariner is thought to have looked in on the peninsula of Castine. In 1605 from Camden came James Rosier, Boswell to Captain Waymouth. The cape at the extreme southwest corner of Brooksville across from Castine harbor bears his name. The Indians had called the point Mose-ka-chick, signifying a moose's rump. The tale is that an Indian was pursuing a moose that came to the shore, jumped in, and started swimming to the other side. The Indian followed in a canoe and succeeded in making the kill. Upon his return he scattered the entrails of the animal in the water, where they may be seen today in the shape of rocks strung along the shore.

In the past four hundred years, Castine has answered to several names: Bagaduce, Pentagoet, and Belfast Bay. The Indians called it Passawamkeag, The Place of the Spirits. As for Bagaduce, this turbulent river divides what was the ancient Pentagoet into two equal parts.

14

In 1614 Captain John Smith referred to French traders in the vicinity, but the first permanent settlement, 1626, was a small development of the Plymouth Colony, a trading post for furs.

In 1632 a French vessel, piloted by a wily Scot and commanded by a Nova Scotian named Rossilon, sailed into the harbor. The captain pretended distress and requested permission to refurbish his vessel. The crew, on first examining the arms of the fort to find they were unloaded, compelled the few on guard to deliver up arms and munition and £500 worth of goods.

Three years later, General Razillai, commander of Acadia, sent Charles de Menou D'Aulnay de Charnissy to capture the trading post. The Plymouth Colony attempted to regain possession, dispatching Captain Girling with the ship *Hope* out of Ipswich. He was accompanied by Myles Standish, who seems to have been guilty of considerable back-seat driving. Standish complained that on reaching gun-shot range there was nothing of consequence left to throw at the scant eighteen men inside the fort. But this was not to be the first time that a superior attacking force was to be paralyzed with buck fever at Castine. Late in 1635 Razillai died. D'Aulnay at Castine and rival La Tour of St. John (New Brunswick) join now in a land and sea feud to outrival the squabbles of the Hatfields and the McCoys. The king of France, up to his ears in the Spanish war, paid little attention to the bloody fight between his officers in far-off New France. D'Aulnay was a Catholic and backed by powerful Jesuits; La Tour, professing to be a Protestant, wooed the support of the Massachusetts Bay Colony.

At one time during the eight-year cat-and-dog fight, La Tour, away on a trip, had left St. John in charge of Madame La Tour, and she, an adequate girl, succeeded in driving off the D'Aulnay forces. D'Aulnay, learning of a second La Tour absence, attacked again and in force. Madame La Tour was obliged to surrender, first having made advantageous terms. D'Aulnay, however, violated the agreement and put the entire garrison to death. Madame La Tour was forced to watch the executions with a rope around her neck; her mental sufferings were too great — she died a few weeks later.

15

Left: Toll bridge connecting Deer Isle with mainland at Sargentville, not as high as the graceful structure over the Penobscot at Bucksport, but very similar in design. Right: Doorway detail at Castine.

Stonington's view points. Islands and quarries in the distance.

Then came a turn of events to rival fiction: D'Aulnay fell out of a rowboat and drowned; the exiled La Tour appeared at Pentagoet, wooed and wed that devastating beauty, his deadly rival's widow, and succeeded to all D'Aulnay's estates. The pair promptly had five children and lived happily thereafter, mostly at St. John.

After 1654 the English, acting under Cromwell, retained for thirteen years undisputed possession of the Castine peninsula, and without molesting the French settlers. Meanwhile the Bay Colony openly traded with the French. "Furnished them [the French]," as Governor Bradford says, "both with provisions and powder and shot; and so continue to do, as they have seen opportunities for their own profit."

Hanging in the Prado is a huge painting by Velásquez, a weaving S-curve composition of cavaliers' lances and impressively caparisoned horses, entitled "The Surrender at Breda." It records the event whereby the English relinquished in 1625 their arms and treaties to the French. The effect of Breda was felt in the New World a year later when the king of England ordered Sir Thomas Temple to yield Pentagoet to the French, "since it represented a stronghold in Acadia."

Accordingly is announced the coming of St. Castin on a Castine billboard: "Here landed August, 1670, the Chevalier de Grande Fontaine, Governor of Acadia, and Baron de St. Castin, his ensign, and other officers, soldiers and savages. Here on this date he received outside its walls the surrender of Fort Pentagoet. . . ." This is the first appearance on the "Maine" scene of one of the most picturesque, most daring cavaliers "who rapped their sword hilts on the portals of New England."

St. Castin, as a member of the regiment Carignan-Salières, at the age of fifteen, according to Longfellow, "had left his chateau in the Pyrenees and sailed across the western seas" to fight with and against the Indians in the forests of Quebec where he learned their dialect and folklore. When the regiment was disbanded, each officer was given "two to three leagues of good land." St. Castin, with broad estates in the Pyrenees, two or three thousand crowns in gold, and an inherited income of five million livres a year, had no need of property. Now he disowns any desire of returning to France, a decision which may have been precipitated by the

16

fact that in Quebec he had been caught cheating at cards. He removes south, officially joins the French investiture at Pentagoet, and soon marries the daughter of Chief Madockawano, a "form of beauty undefined," in the little Catholic church on the island in the Penobscot called Panawamskee, now the site of the present Indian reservation at Old Town. The handsome and generous young officer became a titular divinity to the Indians, and was feared and respected by the English. Not all reports were laudatory. One of the French governors, a Monsieur Perron, seems to have been peculiarly unfriendly; he once detained St. Castin "70 days on a charge of a weakness he had for some females." Yet in 1685, this same Perron borrowed money from St. Castin to purchase two fishing vessels which English fishermen straightway stole from him. Later St. Castin complained that Perron was "retailing brandy by the half pint and not letting any of his domestics do it for him."

Castin also felt the harshness of Sir Edmund Andros, unpopular governor of Massachusetts. When the nobleman and his family were at his father-in-law's island retreat, Andros destroyed and pillaged St. Castin's personal effects. St. Castin nurtured his rage; but it was not until 1695 that he embarked in a flotilla of canoes to join the French under D'Iberville in the attack on Pemaquid.

In 1703 St. Castin departed for France, perhaps meriting Whittier's description:

> In the harsh outlines of his face
> Passion and sin have left their trace;
> Yet, save worn brown and thin grey hair,
> No signs of weary age are there.

This much, however, for the aged Baron's appeal: as the bark cleared the harbor a sorrowing young Indian, Winona, is supposed to have plunged to her death from a cliff above the shore. Castin's son Anselm, his only legitimate offspring, now led the warriors.

In 1840, late in November, a farmer named Grindle was snaking out a wood road near the Penobscot shore. A tree trunk tore a deep rut into the frost-filled soil, snubbing up a shiny French crown; further proddings produced twenty or more pieces. Then darkness closed down, bringing with it the snowflakes of an early season's blizzard. Next morning drifts covered the excavations. It was a long winter for Grindle, who nonetheless could keep a secret. In April he excavated almost two thousand coins — small fractions of crowns and dollars, French money, and Spanish "cob" dollars; a number of Belgian and Portuguese coins, several Massachusetts Pine Tree shillings, and a few English sixpences of 1652 date. Some were irregular in shape and yet of full weight. Could this have been the "good dry gold" left behind by St. Castin when fleeing upstream from Colonel Church's English soldiers near the close of the seventeenth century?

During the Revolution the British were suffering from the attacks of American shipping operating out of Castine. In 1779 they determined to dam up the Yankee flow of provisions, and establish a military post at Bagaduce. General McLean left Halifax with about seven hundred men and landed without opposition. The news brought quick reaction from the merchants of Boston.

Without informing the Continental Congress, the General Court of Massachusetts engaged nineteen armed vessels and twenty-four transports under command of Commodore Gurdon Saltonstall of New Haven, Connecticut. Paul Revere, commissioned a Lieutenant Colonel, left his horse behind, came along as ordnance

Old hoist fragment at Stonington and a Blue Hill smithy and ironworker.

officer in charge of the ammunition; ignominiously, he would return later to his smithy. General Lovell, former Brigadier General of Suffolk militia, guided the land forces, an entirely undisciplined group who had only once paraded together.

On the twenty-fifth, a brisk cannonading began at the river mouth while the Americans effected their first landing. Meanwhile, the huge American fleet maneuvered across the bay just beyond musket shot of the enemy. Sir John Moore, then a British lieutenant, whose burial at Corunna, Spain, ten years later inspired the immortal first lines by Charles Wolfe, "Not a drum was heard, not a funeral note," was on picket when the American land attack was made.

Sir John is not to be confused with the British Captain Moore of the *Margaretta* Incident, the first naval battle of the Revolution, which took place at Machias in 1775. Moore, convoying some lumber ships with a cargo for British barracks at Boston, had aroused the Machias citizens by leveling their liberty pole. On the Sunday following, Moore, while at services, noted patriots surrounding the church. He jumped out of the window and escaped momentarily to his armed vessel on the river. Machias patriots led by five O'Brien brothers boarded the *Margaretta*. While his fiancée awaited him ashore, Moore was carried mortally wounded to the historic Burnham Tavern, Machias, which is still standing.

Despite his 340 guns, Saltonstall now suddenly refused to fight and would not co-operate with Lovell's and Brewer's land forces. In answer to their pleadings, he is reported to have lifted his long chin in the air replying, "You seem to be d —— d knowing about the matter. I am not going to risk my shipping in the d —— d hole." His only action was to send special messengers in whaleboats to Boston for assistance. (Could he have meant sailboats?)

Meanwhile, General Lovell was advancing the hard way, erecting batteries and zigzagging entrenchments. About the time Lovell had achieved the rear of Fort George, a reconnoitering vessel brought intelligence that the British fleet was standing up in the bay. Saltonstall at once ordered an all-over retreat.

Previously one little flurry of victory had occurred during the night when Captain

18

Detail: The blacksmith's lucky pieces.

Little of the American sloop-of-war *Winthrop* captured an armed British brig. Forty Americans, dressed in white frocks in order to distinguish friend from foe, had jumped aboard. Being taken for another English vessel they were casually greeted, "You will run aboard?"

"I am coming aboard," answered Captain Little, and immediately Lieutenant (afterwards the great commodore) Edward Preble with fourteen men sprang up on the deck of the brig. The rest missed their opportunity, owing to the speed of the vessel. At this Captain Little called back hectically, "Will you have more men?" and Preble shouted loudly so as to be heard below decks, "No, we have more than we want, we stand in each other's way." The bluff paid off. The greater part of the enemy's crew leaped overboard and swam to the shore, but Lieutenant Preble made

19

Her Majesty's Canadian cruiser *Quebec* off the Cranberry Islands at Bar Harbor, and, right, the Black house ("Woodlawn") at Ellsworth. The house is open to the public and looks the same as when Colonel Black moved into it.

several officers prisoners in their beds. While English troops on the shore fired upon them, the Americans succeeded in getting the brig safely out of the harbor and to Boston.

Otherwise things were not so good.

By August 4, the British fleet had appeared in the river — seven vessels with 204 guns and 1530 men — to add to three sloops-of-war already in the harbor. Sir George Collier, who had previously received his lumps in a fracas with the inspired defenders of Machias, was in command of the British armada. Now he pompously strutted the bridge of his flagship, which bore the happy name of *The Blonde*. Collier, appreciating his vast superiority in ships and guns, fired broadside upon broadside at the hapless Americans. Crippled by salvos, *The Hunter* was beached with all sails standing. The *Defiance* ran into an inlet nearby and was fired by her crew. The *Sky Rocket* was blown up near Fort Point Ledge; *The Active* went up in flames near Brigadier's Island. Those ships that escaped further up the river were eventually fired or else blown up.

And so a comparatively small British garrison, supplemented only by three sloops-of-war had held out for twenty-one days against a superior force. Probably Saltonstall had been overzealous in volunteering for the assignment. He had taken a fine record into the battle — and he may have fallen prey to the overcautiousness of age. He was charged, however, with having "been bought with British gold," tried and found guilty of cowardice, and cashiered from the service.

The British retained possession of Castine until after the Revolution. All rations were issued by the English commissary. Small change became so scarce that the British commander ordered all silver dollars to be cut into five pieces, each to pass current for one shilling, but so much skullduggery occurred that the order was rescinded. The winter of 1779-80 was probably the coldest ever known in the vicinity. The bay was frozen over; one Lieutenant Burton came all the way from Camden on the ice.

Two years after well bedeviling the British at the unfortunate battle of 1779,

20

Left: The Tarn, Bar Harbor, one of at least twelve bodies of fresh water on Mount Desert Island. Top: A view from summit of Mount Cadillac. Bottom left: Dragger at Southwest Harbor, Mount Desert Island. Bottom right: Sardine carrier with clipper bow was once yacht belonging to pistol-toting Harry K. Thaw.

General Peleg Wadsworth was placed in command of the district of Maine. Shortly thereafter, a Tory informed the British at Castine of the General's retirement whereabouts at Thomaston. One cold February night, the General and his wife were awakened by bullets crashing through their windowpanes. His arm fractured by a ball, the general nonetheless returned the fire. He was summarily captured and removed to Fort George at Castine.

On arrival Wadsworth was treated with every military courtesy. His arm was set and cared for, he was supplied with books and invited to the evening table of the commandant, and for a time his wife and her friend, a Miss Fenno of Boston, were admitted daily. Later he was billeted with a fellow American, Major Burton, whose sloop had been captured by a privateer working off Monhegan Island.

After a few uneventful weeks, the two prisoners gained the intelligence that, since they were rebels of great consequence, plans had been set in motion to deport them to England. In desperation, they managed to obtain a gimlet and bored holes in

21

Spinnaker reach on the Northeast Harbor cruise, a three-day sailing spectacle in late August held off Mount Desert Island.

the pine ceiling, which they concealed in the daytime by plugging them with bread fragments. The perfect night arrived. During the noises of a thunderstorm, they climbed through the ceiling and, between flashes of lightning, made staccato dashes to the riverbank and escaped across the Penobscot.

In 1812 Castine was assailed for a second time by the British, but on this occasion there was no organized Yankee resistance. Just for good measure, Lieutenant Lewis and his forty men fired one volley, then spiked the guns, blew up the redoubt, and escaped up the Penobscot.

A large detachment of British troops marched up the river road, bent on capturing the *John Adams,* a beautiful corvette sitting on the ways undergoing repairs at

22

Hampden. The Americans trained the *Adams'* guns on the oncoming British who proceeded at double-quick through the thick fog; the local militia discharged a few rounds in opposition, then fled to the woods. Betwixt curses and tears, Lieutenant Morris, commanding officer of the *Adams,* set fire to his vessel and took off after his men.

Bangor was spared only on the most humiliating terms. Quarters had to be given the troops, cattle were killed, pork and vegetables, bread and liquor, and all available ammunition provided; between Hampden and Bangor the aggregate booty amounted to about $100,000. Bond was given that the numerous vessels under construction would be delivered in Castine in the spring; all those capable of carrying arms were forced to sign themselves on as prisoners of war.

Castine now became the center of considerable gaiety and activity. On the second of January 1815, the first play was presented at the Theatre Royal, which was a barn fitted up for the performance. The actors, who belonged to the British garrison, gave fortnightly performances; the scenery, decorations, costumes were brought from Halifax.

Dalhousie University in Halifax, Nova Scotia, founded in 1818, was endowed with funds collected at Castine during the occupation of 1812-14. A monument on the campus attests to the fact with the following inscription: "Halifax and Castine. In September 1814, a British naval and military expedition from Halifax under Lieutenant General Sir John Cospe Sherbrooke and Rear Admiral Edward Griffith occupied the portion of Maine between the Penobscot and St. Croix Rivers. Major General Gerard Gosselin governed that district until April 26, 1815. The customs duties collected during this period were utilized by Governor Dalhousie for the endowment of the Garrison Library and Dalhousie College."

Castine's spirits revived with the departure of the English, the precise date the twenty-eighth of April 1815 — a happy day and night. The town was illuminated as bravely as the shortage of gas or coal oil would permit. Many of the houses were lighted by candles stuck in potatoes.

Castine, having weathered the antagonisms of the British, likewise had to endure the general run of crimes and abnormalities of any other community. Some of them are worth recording.

On the formation of Hancock County, in 1790, Penobscot was made a shire town. After 1801, one term of the Supreme Court was held there each year. Ten years later, one Ebenezer Ball of Deer Isle was sentenced to be hanged for the murder of a sheriff, who, it seems, had apprehended him while passing counterfeit money.

Dr. Mose Adams, of Ellsworth, was tried in Castine for the ax-murder of his wife — a direct hit on the jugular. The physician was seen shortly after the estimated time of the kill busily walking up the road away from the scene, looking over his shoulder toward the house. However, Judge Mellen, attorney for Adams, submitted that what could be more natural, for the doctor, who was a fast walker, to turn around occasionally to face any little breeze that might be blowing. The prisoner was acquitted for lack of evidence. This trial is perhaps best remembered because at one point in the proceedings the second story gallery collapsed under the overcrowded weight of curious spectators.

An Indian named Moosup was once tried for the murder of a barkeep from Bangor. Chief Neptune of the Penobscot tribe arose in Castine court and with great dignity declaimed, "One God made us all. You know your people do my

Left: The fish "bailer" at McKinley, Mount Desert Island, a picturesque method now replaced by mechanical means. Right: Entrance to a fish weir. Tide and twigs conspire to trap the silvery sardine.

Indians great deal wrong. You murder them — then they walk right off; nobody touches them. . . . Peace is good. . . . These, my Indians, smile under its shade. The great Spirit is our Father. . . . I speak what I feel." Neptune, in full Indian regalia, provided a dramatic contrast to the Judge Advocate, wearing the court dress of the period. Moosup was bound in $500 and a year's good behavior.

A "haunted" cellar in an old house in Castine earned its reputation. It seems that an Indian servant, without her mistress's knowledge, made a habit of leaving her infant in the old-fashioned stone oven for its afternoon nap. One afternoon the housewife, not knowing of the unique siesta practice, took it upon herself to do some baking. According to the old report: "In short order there was a quantity of roast papoose."

Castine's public library, the first in Maine, had been founded in 1801. In 1875 the Castine Minstrel Club was formed for the purpose of raising funds for new books. Among the Castinettes, there was apparently a reverence for the "Athens of America" 250 miles down the coast, for an aged and ailing bluestocking told her doctor in 1850 "that she wanted to go to Heaven by way of Boston."

Longfellow never saw the Nova Scotia site of his poem *Evangeline,* and, although he wrote a poem of St. Castin, he never journeyed to Castine. Not so for his brother Alexander Longfellow, however. His life's work involved a geodetic survey of the coast of Maine, while other members of the Longfellow family, as well as the Whittiers, became early summer residents. About 1879, John Greenleaf Whittier also kicked in with a poem on St. Castin and his gorgeous Indian bride.

The quiet dignified atmosphere of Castine attracted a conservative element. A local historian reports in the eighties "that it has come down to the present time a happy family of refined, educated vacationists, carrying a fairly well equalized purse and enjoying the benefits of mutual association without any of the heart-burnings caused by rivalry."

With the exception of Ben Ames Williams, who treated Castine briefly in *The*

24

Somes Sound, one of the few warm salt-water swimming sites off Mount Desert Island.

Strange Woman and *Come Spring,* exponents of the "Maine story" have somehow avoided a historical novel with Castine as the background. Neither James Oliver Curwood nor Arthur Somers Roche, who summered at Castine, made the town the subject of any important manuscript. Roche struck literary paydirt long after he had left the peninsula, a sorrowful departure, for he had lost the beautiful young Castine-born wife at the birth of their son.

Harriet Beecher Stowe and her son, the Reverend Charles, sojourned in Castine for several summers. The ladies of the town felt that Mrs. Stowe wore her hair in a rather frowzy style and that there was a slatternly air in the way she put on her clothes. But much could be forgiven the woman who wrote *Uncle Tom's Cabin* and those entertaining stories of Orr's Island. Still a light rancor always lingered because she didn't incorporate Castine in a novel.

III

Bar Harbor and Mount Desert Island

Fire, Ferry and Axe Murders

The Bar Harbor fire of October, 1947, which according to the official U. S. National Park publications was caused by "carelessness," was an epochal twenty-three million dollar blaze that made the headlines universally. A week or so afterwards, the Bar Harbor public relations man found his way into the New York office of the late Steve Hannegan, publicist extraordinary, known for his successful application of the bathing-girl-on-the-sands technique. Among Hannegan's triumphs was a tub-thumping campaign for Miami Beach which put that resort into its spot in the semi-tropical sun.

"What could be done for the future of Bar Harbor?"

"Nothing," said Mr. Hannegan.

"But," contended the Maine promotion man, who, incidentally, had been accused of setting the fire to get clippings for his press scrapbook, "consider the world-wide publicity accrued from the fire?"

"That's for sure," rejoined the fabulous Hannegan. "Go jump off the Empire State Building. Tomorrow you make page 1. But that's the end."

A Lidice role was not for Bar Harbor, however, and, as it proved out, more tourists have visited the Island since the fire than ever before. More than merely a ghoulish interest keeps them in town today. The old gal still has her looks. The replacement trees — the birches and maples which most always sprout on burnt ground — seven years after the fire were waist high; and the gutted trunks, spectre-like, resembling the gaunt sticks which pass for trees in a Vlaminck snow-scene, will not long remain standing against the winds and erosion.

In Paris at the time of the holocaust, the newspaper *Figaro* reported that the fire had been set by the "peasants" revolting against the large estates. But the other way around would have made more sense. Many of the summer mansion owners, having sweltered since World War I under high taxes levied on outmoded white elephants, were wondering how to get rid of their architectural liabilities short of tearing them down, giving them to the Jackson Memorial Laboratory or The Catholic Church. Then came the fire, and most beneficiaries pocketed their insurance monies and made for the other side of the Island to Newport or Europe. Would they rebuild? What, at current construction prices, and with a local taxation without representation policy based on March Town Meeting votes, and no zoning laws, at least none with teeth. Nice knowing you, thank you very much.

The fire stopped short at Seal, Northeast Harbor and Somesville, and, in fact,

Valhalla waits for the wind off Southwest Harbor, Mount Desert Island.

very few of the front teeth, the shoreline properties of Bar Harbor, are missing. There is plenty of land left on Mount Desert; it is the third or fourth largest island off the continental United States, depending how you count the areas of the bay territory off Puget Sound. And to all judgments Mount Desert is still "The Most Beautiful Island in the World."

The new Bar Harbor-Yarmouth, Nova Scotia Ferry site — unless it goes honky-tonk, should transfuse new blood into the grand old spa. Its 105 mile course across the mouth of the Bay of Fundy, a historic route, followed by our

Bar Harbor, whose streets and vistas often reveal a warship at one end, a mountain at the other.

Acadian explorers from the beginning and saving hundreds of land miles, will be traversed by a 5,000 ton, five million dollar ship tieing up to a several million dollar pier. According to promises, it will be free from the usual waterfront steamer dock blemishes.

Exactly three hundred and fifty years before the Bar Harbor-Yarmouth ferry entered Frenchman's Bay, Sieur de Champlain in 1604, with a few companions in a small lateen rigged bark, coasted down from Port Royal (Annapolis Royal), Nova Scotia, having spent a rugged winter so cold that cider was served by the block on an island between St. Andrews and Calais on the St. Croix River. After being greeted by friendly Indians in canoes, Champlain, who never put foot on shore, named the island Isle des Monts Deserts (this time the Monts signified the bare mountains, not his patron, De Monts). With the appellation "Deserts," he at once confused later generations of tourists with its pronunciation. Call it like the sweet course of a meal or as in the Desert of Sahara; both are right.

During the 17th century, Mount Desert, like the rest of Acadia, from Nova Scotia to Camden, was predominantly French. Another pilgrimage, this one strictly religious, from France via Port Royal, Nova Scotia, arrived on the island in 1613. This was the ill-fated Jesuit expedition. As the boatload of priests, soldiers and sailors slid into Bar Harbor waters, they must have liked what they saw, for according to the "Shadowy purple" visualization of Historian Parkman — "The ship bore on before a favoring wind, foam spouting from beneath her bows as she entered Frenchman's Bay, where dome-like islands rose, green with forests and gray with jutting rocks, with restless waves sparkling and dancing between. The jet-black shadow betwixt crags and sea and pines along the cliff, penciled against the fiery sunset, the dreamy slumber of the distant mountains bathed in shadowy purple — such is the scene. Peace in the wilderness; peace on the sea." Such melodramatic description holds today, nonetheless, doubled and redoubled.

Possibly the soporific beauty of the Somes Sound site lulled the Jesuit mission into the belief that no possibility of man's violence could be abroad. So the French, despite the pleas of a few, settled down on Fernald's Point, forgot fortifications in favor of agriculture, sun baths, and the conversion of the natives. But somehow, Governor Argall of Virginia, seafighter, abductor of Pocahontas, had learned of the Fleur de Lis expedition, and he forthwith appeared with a true Hollywood flourish off Greenings Island, the red flag of England streaming from the masthead, bugles blaring, artillery and small arms roaring. This power-play was completely successful. Those Frenchmen who emerged unscathed were either set afloat in open boats or else taken back with Argall to Virginia. Despite the fact that there was no Bar Harbor-Nova Scotia ferry or other shipping to pick up the abandoned Jesuits, they amazingly made it back to Port Royal.

With the levelling of the inchoate Jesuit mission at Mount Desert, a famous first was established. In this romantic fjord had occurred the first clash of arms between the French and the English, one of the many encounters to continue in Acadia for over one hundred years. Again our authority is Boston's favorite historian-son Francis Parkman: "In a semi-piratical desert, an obscure stroke of lawless violence began the strife of France and England, Protestantism and Rome, which, for a century and a half, shook the struggling communities of North America, and closed at last in the memorable triumph on the Plains of Abraham."

After the extermination of the Jesuits, there were no more Frenchmen of record on the Island until the early seventeen hundreds and the coming of Sieur de Mothe de Cadillac (or Condillac), a publicity-minded Frenchman who later became head of Detroit. Although General Motors may not know it, Cadillac was a roustabout most of his life who had once served time in the Bastille. He lived for a while on Mount Desert Island, charting its waters, claiming it as his seignory and proudly signing his correspondence with the Mount Desert tag. Governor Andros, who often got around Acadia to check in at Castine and other points, reports that Cadillac was living on the Island in 1688. Exactly 100 years later, his granddaughter, Madame Térèse de Gregoire, settled in Hull's Cove, having first, with an adroit feminine positiveness that cannot be underestimated, persuaded a covey of important gentlemen — including the Marquis de Lafayette, Monsieur Otto, the Ambassador to the United States, Thomas Jefferson and Benjamin Franklin, and in fact the entire General Court of Massachusetts — that at least half the Island deserved to be hers. She and her husband, Barthélémy, played host to Indians and a rather constant French monk; and apparently there were some gay parties among their fishermen neighbors, with an occasional variation in the form of an orgy on rum and molasses. When Mme. de Gregoire died, a belt of solid gold was found around her waist. The pair were buried at Hull's Cove, and for some years only a wooden cross marked the de Gregoires' graves, which reputedly were set outside the main cemetery because they were Catholics.

During the Revolution, Bar Harbor, then called Eden, at one time surrendered to the British; in fact, in 1781 the British sloop of war *Allegiance,* on its way up Frenchman's Bay, after firing salvos at three white rocks in a fog, having mistaken them for a Yankee schooner — to this day the promontory is called Schooner Head — kept on up the roadstead, destroyed a few houses at Waukeag Neck, and swept off as captives several old militia officers of the 6th Lincoln County Regiment. Richard Hale in *The Story of Bar Harbor*, a recent volume full of distinction and research, alleges that at the time one Edenite was slandered in the British records by the assertion that he offered his daughter to a Marine sergeant for freedom to escape. The sergeant declined — a terrible slur on Maine womanhood!

Probably the first summer colony visitors at Mount Desert and, incidentally, the Island's first publicists, were artists of the celebrated Hudson River School. Thomas Cole, founder of the Group, after painting Penobscot Bay and Castine in 1844, journeyed overland to the Island and discovered more than adequate subjects for his brush and pencil. On the word of Cole, Thomas Birch and Frederick Church and other disciples came to the Island, and, what is more, after returning to the cities sold their paintings to important collections. Thomas Cole named Eagle Lake, one of the several fresh water bodies on the Island, because of the bald eagles which wheeled over his easel; and he said, with demonstration of superior hearing, "One might easily fancy himself in the forests of the Alleghenies, but for the dull roar of the ocean breaking the stillness." Today fishing in Eagle Lake is a full summer's sport. As to its catch, comment is withheld, but Charles Dudley Warner said of the Island's streams, "There must have been many trout here for few are caught."

Alpheus Hardy of Boston, the first long-term summer visitor, built his "cottage" in 1867 (even today the biggest house on the Island is called a "cottage"). Hardy, well ahead of the wave of shore buying for private estates, was surrounded by "rusticators;" these denizens of boarding houses were divided into two classes, "mealers" and "hauled mealers." Some of the impressions of the early boarding houses' occupants have been set down charmingly in an early Mount Desert guide book, copyrighted in 1888 by Hugh Chisholm. He declares that in the old time hotels at Bar Harbor the accommodations were rustic and simple. The rising bell rang at 6:30 and breakfast was served before seven. One complaining guest was answered, "Wal, you came here for a change, didn't you? Now you've got it." To another, who sarcastically asked the boniface who taught him to keep a hotel, the answer was, "The Lord Almighty . . ." A sophisticated New Yorker asked what kind of griddle cakes were those mentioned on the bill of fare. "Well, I call them fust rate," calmly said the table-girl. General complaints were made of the fried

Left: Hefting the herring — inside the sardine weir. Right: Veteran of Corea, Maine — lobsterman, his face tanned like leather from the sun and the whip of the winds.

meat supplied, and the housekeeper exclaimed, "Fried fresh beef is good 'nuff for me and the cap'n and I guess it's good enough for them starched up city folks. We've allus eat it that way, and them city folks ain't no healthier than we be." Another metropolitan guest suggested, "Mr. Landlord, I shall put my boots outside my door tonight." And the hearty old Innkeeper roared out, "All right, sir, you'll find 'em there in the morning, we're all honest folk around here."

Charles Dudley Warner, who wrote entertainingly of Cape Breton Island in "Baddeck, and That Sort of Thing," said en route to Nova Scotia, "Bar Harbor has one of the most dainty and refined little hotels in the world, The Malvern. Anyone can stay there who is worth two millions of dollars, or can produce a certificate from the recorder of New York that he is a direct descendant of Hendrick Hudson or Diedrich Knickerbocker." The Malvern, like so many other Bar Harbor wooden hotels, fell in ashes in the Fire of 1947.

With the arrival of the gay nineties, Bar Harbor had become a social capital of the United States. There were those who bewailed the fashionable conquest and the change from fish and skeleton chickens at $5 a week, to reed birds, lobsters and sweetbreads and champagne at $5 a day, from rocking and mountain climbing to musicales and lawn parties. Chisholm reports that it was too much for a Miss Ellen Robbins, a flower painter. She sold her cottage, moved away, saying, "If I were to come again next year, I should expect to see the rocks and trees all decorated with lace flowers and bows of ribbons." General Frémont, the famous Pathfinder of the West, bought one of the Porcupine Islands in Frenchman's Bay, but found its possession a dubious utility and allowed it to be sold for taxes.

At the turn of the century, Charles W. Eliot, President Emeritus of Harvard, and perhaps the earliest summer resident of Northeast Harbor, in concert with his landscape architect son, Charles W. Eliot, Jr., felt a positive fear that the natural beauty of the Island, a community asset which he realized must be preserved for the financial good of the inhabitants, was endangered. Indiscriminate lumbering, the sad appearances of some of the village areas gave rise to thoughts even more acute than those of William Cullen Bryant when twenty years before in "Picturesque America" he had decried the expedient ugliness of this tourist-mad community. Besides, the portable saw had just been invented, and the verdant mountain tops, hitherto inaccessible to the axe, were in jeopardy. Spurred on by his son, who understood the advantages of available public domains and who had formed a highly successful Massachusetts Trustees of Public Reservations, Eliot père eventually interested George Dorr, kindly and effective Boston bachelor, in establishing for the Island and for the country at large, the Acadia National Park, the first National Park east of the Mississippi. Whereas islanders once objected to the park because it took lands off the tax rolls, today the city fathers bless Messrs. Eliot, Dorr and Rockefeller for having protected for all time one of nature's best efforts — an asset defying all monetary estimates in net worth as a vacation attraction.

For an example of an axe murder committed in the name of expediency witness the wounds of the 1953 lumbering of Bar Island opposite the town's municipal wharf. One half the celebrated island is part of Acadia National Park and so in contrast, remains inviolate; its solid spruces stare down on the stumps of their less fortunate brothers like those state witnesses who are forced to look upon a death house execution.

John Marin at Cape Split, Addison, Maine, interrupts Bach for a long-time exposure.

IV

Aestheticism in Washington County:
Adam Architecture; John Marin

IN WASHINGTON COUNTY, noted for "the best fishing and hunting in the United States," one may go loaded for deer in season but seldom for Adam architecture or modern art — the old Ruggles House at Columbia Falls and John Marin, painter, at Cape Split.

Proceeding through the blueberry country: Columbia Falls edges the road so briefly that one speeds through the town and out within a few seconds. Not, however, without first noting "the house." Sitting upon the apron of a curve on Route 1, how it has escaped being knocked awry by a hurrying truckload of sardines or lobsters is a miracle.

The late Arthur Train, writer, creator of the Yankee lawyer, Mr. Tutt, discovered the old gem years ago at a time when it was barely visible through the bushes that covered its façade. Train employed the house as the theme of one of his best short stories, the second page of which contained this sentence: "In its reminiscence of an exotic elegance and its wistful charm, it was like the ghost of a dainty old lady dressed in gray silk, who, having wandered out of the past, had sat down by the roadside and forgotten to go back." Train did more than write about the house; he and Richard Hale gamely tried to interest Bar Harbor friends in its preservation.

The gray color has been replaced by a harder coat of white; the house, now open to the public, and boasting better support than before, is more than ever an architectural beauty receiving compliments. Distinguished architects of modern times, we are told, have stood before it in amazement and declared that nowhere have they seen its like. Perhaps it's not that good, but it is certainly worth spending six minutes within its four small rooms and stepping over its unbelievably beautiful flying double staircase, which rises, vaporishly thin, from the center of the hall and then divides into two half-flights without any lateral support to the landing. One unencumbered worshiper speaks of the little staircase as having the "sheer grace and lightness of a bird beginning to soar." In the living room, the fireplace mantel shows mahogany beneath the white paint, where a carver had many a field day cutting lozenge patterns.

Supposedly the house was built and designed by Aaron Sherman, "pattern maker," who had been born in Duxbury, Massachusetts, in 1798. He was versed in the stolid building traditions handed down from the Plymouth Colony; yet here at Columbia Falls, four hundred miles from his native Massachusetts' South Shore, an equally rough salt-marsh country, he has worked in a style of architecture that is delicacy to a degree. It is believed that there are other Sherman examples in Columbia Falls and in Machias, fifteen miles away, but none have enjoyed the special handling and eventual recognition of the Ruggles House.

The style of the house is generally called "Adam," that early mode of classicism whose most notable practitioner in America was Charles Bulfinch. Among the carpenter builders who employed its use, the name of McIntyre of Salem figures prominently, and Sherman, apparently, was no insignificant follower. Probably this house at Columbia Falls was his most important work, and he designed and constructed it for the most influential man in the town — Thomas Ruggles, lumber and shipping king, a man whose word was "yea and amen" among all who had dealings with him.

About the time Ruggles was appointed judge of the court sitting at Machias, he had expressed the desire to build commensurate with his importance. There is a legend that an unknown English carver, whose "knife was guided by an angel," was imprisoned three years in the house, creating with penknife the intricate petals and furbelows of wood, the graceful ribbon streamers that loop over the windows, the delicate urns, the caps of the porch column and the veining of the leaves. (Three years may have been not too long a time for such arduous work. In later days another craftsman, employed to duplicate a small section of damaged beading edging a panel, required fifteen evenings to accomplish the task.) The name of the mysterious carver appears in none of the town records or newspaper reports. It could have been that Aaron Sherman did the wood carving as well as the building.

Ruggles lived only briefly in his dream dwelling, but a descendant, Mary Ruggles Chandler, a great-granddaughter, almost a hundred years later became its guardian angel. For a time she had dwelt in the old house and by day worked in the village pharmacy next door. When the drugstore burned to the ground, destroying all of her father's and grandfather's rare surgical instruments, Miss Chandler fought with her hands to keep the adjacent Ruggles House from going up in the flames. Although more than once desperately in need, Miss Chandler refused to sell the house's most outstanding architectural feature, the fantastic flying stair-

34

Left: Adam Architecture — the old Ruggles House at Columbia Falls.

Right: Miss Chandler, custodian and Ruggles kin, as rare a personality as the house itself, framed by the graceful flying double staircase with its solid mahogany newel posts and rails.

Right: Signature for which collectors of modern art have paid thousands, here delineated against a Maine fog.

case. One philanthropist who sought to present the stairs to the Metropolitan Museum of New York for its American Wing, offered $10,000.

Miss Chandler, the first licensed woman pharmacist in Maine, is as much a personality as the house itself. She often reads Shakespeare with her friend Dr. Josephine Leighton, former professor at Columbia in New York, who still corrects theses and other papers for the university.

"It was all right," says Miss Chandler when she remembers how, years ago, she had to forego college and a career as a doctor because she was obliged to earn her living as a pharmacist, "Had I gone away I would not have been able to watch over the house."

To have stumbled on this urbane expression of architectural taste 250 miles from Portland and almost to the Canadian border seems surprising enough. But, striking down seven miles to Addison on Cape Split, we come face to face with an even more amazing spectacle of art in the wilderness.

Here, in summers, works the ultramodern artist John Marin, American, among the rugged boulders of marsh and forest, where the great tides sweep in and around the spruce and granite islands. His style is quite apart from the Norman Rockwell school, and therefore he is not known to the typical reader of the *Saturday Evening Post*.

On a fog-laden road running between a soft aisle of dripping spruces, suddenly there was the famous signature, for which museums and esoteric collectors have paid thousands — John Marin. But this time on a battered mailbox.

He was waylaid on his piazza, playing on his ancient Chickering grand piano. In the glassed-in, dreary light he held still for a time exposure, at least for a full second. Rooting his basketball-type shoes firmly on the piazza boards, he let the cruel lens penetrate his features, a face of curious lines and areas of sensitive expression, as different from the average run as a Marin is from other works of art. Not on Fifty-Seventh Street but nonetheless in Manhattan, Marin's avuncular dealer, Alfred Stieglitz, celebrated photographer, for years had shown Marin in his gallery, called An American Place. Stieglitz was the husband of Georgia O'Keeffe, famous introspective artist who, like as not, will paint the skull of a steer or a stupendous calla lily in one or more canvasses. Stieglitz always commanded the highest prices for Marins; like diamonds, he never released them in volume, and always made sure that they fell into strong hands.

In his early days Marin worked in an architect's office. Later he rendered engravings and silver points in as meticulous a manner as Méryon, Whistler, or Pennell. Today, his approach is something else. Whether or not you understand Marin, everyone can appreciate his technical wizardry in the sureness and clarity with which he applies the trickling pigment. "As a water colorist he is supreme," Albert Eugene Gallatin said, "you would have to travel back to the ancient Chinese masters to find his equal." Most of the big shots of art consider Marin our greatest modern painter, as sincere and proficient, as much an American master, as was John Singleton Copley or Winslow Homer. Others, not so understanding, feel that Marin's message is a little like that whistle that only the dogs can hear.

Marin isn't attempting to copy slavishly the world which he so basically loves. He cannot give us a literal transcript. Nature hits him harder than the rest of us mortals. He isn't merely holding up some film as any one of us can do to mirror nature and then let Mr. Eastman Kodak or Rolleiflex do the rest. He portrays his emotion by emphasizing here and distorting there, yet keeping the whole in balance, like the plan for a Japanese garden. Marin's triangular jabs are like the effects produced by dropping a naked pane of glass on the floor — the tormented forms blend into a design pattern of solid relationship, each part to the other.

We can best understand the man, perhaps, in his letters to Stieglitz, many of which he signed puckishly "That ancient Mariner, John Marin." This relationship, which might be construed as that of patron and remittance man yet in effect amounting to something considerably more important, is revealed in the collected writings of Marin edited by Dorothy Norman and in his biography by MacKinley Helm. Marin insisted that Stieglitz always let him alone to work. There was no parallel like that of the wood carver, restrained, some believe, three years in the Ruggles House until his job was done. Stieglitz realized that Marin would voluntarily segregate himself summers in wild remote country, just as Picasso, while selling to the tycoons of industry, nevertheless lived by choice in a ramshackle château in rustic France, where he revelled in using Renaissance lamps fitted with oil wicks. Marin in winters has of late lived outside New York City, across the Hudson; the towered city pleases him better from the distant palisades of New Jersey.

When Marin first came to West Addison on Cape Split, he at once felt right at home. "After all," as he has said in one of his letters, "I am only a small town gink with a small town disposition."

36

Marin waves to friend in the Jonesport-type boat. Named *The Bidu Sayao* for the opera singer who summered at Cape Split.

When we were well into the late war, one of his letters suggested that he could consider a year-round existence on Cape Split. The very next winter a German submarine was to thread the underwater passages of Frenchman's Bay and land two spies at Hancock Point, twenty miles down the coast from Addison.

By now the fog had lifted. He posed before his easel down on the rocks. A Jonesport-type lobster boat slid by. Marin the "gink" waved his brush aloft and an equally responsive salute came from a Wass or Thompson neighbor. The name on the bow of the "Jonesy" boat was *Bidu Sayao*. The Metropolitan Opera star had spent one summer on the cape, and she was to be remembered well beyond the plaudits of the diamond horseshoe with this appraisal of a Maine fisherman.

The painter made a few passes at his canvas. Confidentially a young hand covered a quick area of lines and shapes that to me resembled not at all the scene it confronted. Marin is a fast worker. "Like golf," he says, "the fewer strokes I take the better." Meanwhile the sunlight was improving and the warmth of the afternoon declaring itself. The dark tide looked inviting in the stillness. The remoteness of the place, the vitality of the salt air made one desire to strip off clothes and sprint via the water route — the colder the better — to the nearest island.

Twine before pearls. Studying the dawn haul. Sometimes the herring scale used for processed jewelry is worth more than the sardines themselves.

V

Toward Lubec and Eastport: The Sardine Sea

THE PUBLIC at large seldom is confronted with the spectacle of a school of herring, or sardines as they call them in Maine. According to a front page story in the New York *Herald Tribune,* at a place called Glenwood Landing, there occurred an unwanted herring run that almost shut down the turbines of the Long Island Lighting Company's 300,000 kilowatt plant. For more than a week the company assigned men to scoop twelve tons of herring off intake screens through which sea water passed, before cooling the steam from the turbines in the condensers.

An aquatic biologist of the state identified the fish as round herring and surmised that they were produced by a prolific spawning coupled with favorable feeding conditions. He also believed that the fish were attracted by light and advised the plant to shut off its waterfront lights at night.

A Down Easter doesn't have to be an icthyologist to know that the sardine swims in surface waters at night and therefore is particularly attracted by artificial light. "Torching" — the water equivalent of jacking deer by flashlight — has been prohibited by law for several decades.

On the Maine coast until recent times facilities have not always been available to handle gargantuan catches. When Castine in 1908 had its record run — a brush weir in the Bagaduce River took twenty million small herring — it was a quantity so large for that date that no local market could be found and the catch had to be sent to places as far eastward as Lubec. Catches the size of the historic Castine pack would be absorbed today within thirty-six hours.

It is rare, however, for schools of herring to sally forth farther south than Cape Cod. They are never caught commercially south of Block Island. They have been known to get as far south as New Jersey, but only in the cold weather.

The name sardine derives from the dim past when considerable quantities were taken off the Mediterranean Island of Sardinia.

The famous Norwegian product falls into two classes: the brisling, a North Sea herring; and the sild, quite another species of fish. The "true sardine" category, many experts declare, can be applied only to the French or Portuguese variety. Some of the U.S. packers, however, in Lubec for instance, will contest that the Maine sardine is every bit as "true" as the imported. The Maine sardines are all herrings and considered "immature" up to nine inches. The Californian sardine, a distinct species, is often referred to as the pilchard.

The Atlantic herring is about 3½ inches long at one year, 5½ inches at two,

Left: As seen through a broken lobster trap, a Jonesport lobster boat. Right: Swimming pool, Jonesport style — one of the town's large lobster pounds.

7½ inches at three, 8½ inches at four, 9½ inches at five, 10½ inches at six, 11½ inches at seven, 12 inches at eight, and only grows another inch during the following four years. The first spawning period is in the third year, and almost all have spawned by the fifth year.

There has been the constant fear that vast schools of sardines might shift with their feeding grounds from long-used locations, and that overnight a million-dollar industry would go out with the tide. However, the Maine coast, because of the unique spawning and protective mechanism supplied by the tidal surge of the Passamaquoddy Bay area, looks right now to be the safest bet for long continued sardine fishing, unless there is a major geologic upheaval.

The area may have missed out selling to the nation those turbulent Fundy tides for hydroelectric power, but it would seem that the Maine sardine industry has been blessed by a phenomenon of nature which to and fro titilates the plant life and sweeps the small herring, the sardine, into an area where he can grow to succulent size, "fat in the gut, and fat in the meat," protected from his enemies of deeper channels — the cod, the silver hake, the squid, the dogfish.

The salt- and fresh-water mix caused by the great rivers pouring into the gulf of Maine and New Brunswick — such as the St. John, St. Croix, the Narraguagus, the Penobscot, the Georges, and the Kennebec — apparently provide the perfect water blend for the existence of plant life on which the herring feed.

Huxley, the celebrated English scientist of a few decades past, stated that the North Atlantic herring will be around for a long time despite being constantly preyed upon by whales, porpoises, and sea animals both large and small, and such fish as cod and mackerel, and even by bird-kingdom members like gulls and gannets. Huxley advocated the belief that, even if only two of the 20,000 progeny of a female herring spawn, this North Atlantic species will not readily disappear. He says, "Man, in fact, is but one of a vast cooperative society of herring-catchers . . . if man took none, the other shareholders would have a larger dividend and would thrive and multiply in proportion, but it would come to pretty much the

"The Sea — that's my occupation." When this solid character was about ten years old a boatload of Jonesporters sailed in a 600-ton bark on a pilgrimage to Palestine, the strangest religious exodus and example of mass hypnosis New England has ever seen. Taken in by a fanatical leader, whose shipboard services grew constantly incoherent, and who advised, "Drink rum, brethren, and abide with God," only a handful survived the horrible rigors of the desert.

same thing to the herrings." However, Huxley's optimistic North Sea theories seem to obtain not at all in respect to the *Clupea pallasii,* the herring of the North Pacific. The explanation for this disappearance in California seems to be overfishing.

Soon after the turn of the century the West Coast sardine catch was found to be heavy in oil. California conservation authorities insisted that the sardine industry shift to the producing of whole fish to be used as meal for fertilizer. Then, about 1920, the law was changed, stipulating that for every ton of fish there must be twelve cases of sardines — the balance to be processed into meal and oil. Year after year the authorities set a new figure; and subsequently the fishery was conducted farther out to sea. What had happened to the mackerel — inshore extinction — now befell the sardine.

After thirty or more years of diminishing fishing without too much attention to the letter of the law, the California conservation groups began to feel that perhaps they had not been tough enough. Contrary to lay belief, it has become a universal conservation practice in the sardine world to leave the bigger ones because the seniors are the most active breeders. Some time ago the lobster industry accepted this truism. That is why the taking of gargantuan lobsters is prohibited in Maine.

In the ocean's scheme of things, most of its animals feed on other fish at least one size smaller. The herring, however, a defenseless little fish, has no brothers below him — only the plankton life. In the plankton world the same bigger-eat-smaller mechanism continues, for the copepods feed on the diatoms. Where the cod is we have this chain of nourishment; and likewise we have the great fisheries such as the Grand Bank of Newfoundland and waters like those along the coast of Maine which are rich in phosphates and nitrates.

How much nutriment will man eventually absorb directly from the polar ice? The essential mineral content of the sea world is a study within itself.

But these so-called fertilizer salts of the North Atlantic make up the diet for the fussy little diatoms, the plankton, on which all fish life depends. These northern waters, of course, are fed by the Labrador current that rises in the Arctic and flows south along the Atlantic seaboard.

The cod cruises most happily over his vast ocean preserve. He belongs to a very large family; for each cod lays four million eggs yearly, although without too much thought of their security, scattering them helter-skelter to the deep currents.

42

Left: Each Jonesport street sign proudly bears the silhouette of a "Jonesy" boat.
Right: Birdhouse; more ornate than Jonesport dwellings themselves.

Top: Herring smokehouse at Bailey's Mistake.
Left: Tidewater scene, Jonesport. Right: "Dried pollock makes a right nice meal."

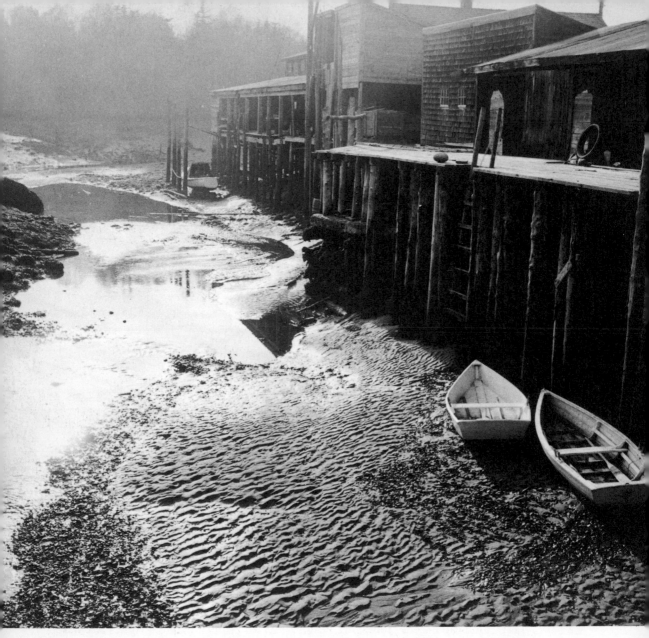

Back lighting at Bailey's Mistake, named by a fog-ridden mariner who fetched the wrong harbor.

The female herring lays only about 20,000 eggs, attaching them in poorly ventilated clumps to the rocks and shoals of shallow water. The bottom-laying method of the herring, producing demersal eggs (the cod lays pelagic eggs), has two advantages: there is security from deep-water enemies such as the silver hake, the squid, and the cod, and the inshore nursery feeding grounds prevent the deep currents from washing them too soon into offshore areas where existence is more difficult.

The herring eggs, about one-twentieth of an inch across, appear huge when compared with the miniature eggs of the copepods, those small crustaceans on

44

With an oar, line, or other gimmick he can tell the exact size of the catch to a hogshead (17½ bushels). The tube sucks up the sardines and simultaneously separates their silvery scales, the latter to be processed eventually into synthetic pearls. Constricting the purse seines — great physical strength is essential.

which it exists. (A lobster is a crustacean, but it is several thousand times larger than the items on which the herring feed. Then there are copepods and certain small shrimps, all members of minute sea life known as "plankton.") Eventually these fishlets' embryos swim toward the surface, where food is more plentiful, feeding on their own yolk sacs as they go. We hail, among other authorities, N. J. Berrill, author of *The Living Tide,* for valuable information about herring.

To say that the cod love herring is an understatement. Fact is that the cod chases the herring on both sides of the North Atlantic. Unfortunately, for the herring, the cod, too, likes cold water; for neither of them is found in temperatures

Lubec: The rich crimson and white bands of West Quoddy Head light. Farthest east point in the United States.

above fifty-five degrees. Fortunately for the "babies" their early inclination is to stay near shore and away from the deeper happy hunting grounds of the cod.

More herring go down the throat of the cod than any other fish, but he does not subsist on a diet solely of herring. Not overchoosy, apparently the cod is just as cannibalistic as the lobster, who often lives on his own progeny. One icthyologist callously observes, "The habit probably has value from an evolutionary point of view, by helping to weed out the poorer swimmers before they can grow and reproduce."

Whereas the cod feeds on the herring, the herring feeds on the calanus (red feed) and the calanus in turn on the diatoms, smallest organisms of the sea. In search of its food, the minute herring speed along in a manner very like the whale, force feeding out particles of the plankton life. It swims with his mouth open, water streaming through its gills and past the gill rakers, while the nourishing diatoms,

46

green-colored and vitamin-packed, actually chlorophyll, are strained into its stomach. Each fall whales, searching for herring schools, appear in the Bay of Fundy.

As for the method of catch: Down East the little Sardine was originally taken in weirs, an aboriginal device.

The weir, always pronounced "wear," can be described as a conglomeration of poles and nets, a corral half under water and half above. There are numerous variations of these structures, and there are weirs for incoming and outgoing tides. Weirs may be seen by the coastal traveler protruding from many a Maine cove or bay, looking as if a line of bracken bushes were growing out of the water.

Once the herring enters the weir, he doesn't have the wit to swim out the way he came in, and, of course, the tide is giving him a push in the direction he is supposed to take. Left too long in a weir — say more than two days — the herring, helped on by the alternate tides, contrives to escape.

One autumn a Sorrento weir owner elected sport on land in favor of commercial fishing. He thus lost $10,000, when, in his absence, his weir filled and emptied at least three times. Often the State of Maine fisherman will decide on a full week's deer hunting, disregarding the potential revenue the silvery catch may represent.

A pocket net is set within the large twine and now the fish are collected closely together and are ready for the insertion of a canvas scoop, a sort of dip net, called the bailer, manipulated from a hoist.

Weirs are fortuitous investments only if there is not too great an expense involved in their building. They generally cost between three and five thousand dollars. In the erecting of a weir, many a shrewd fisherman farmer will hope to work along with his neighbor or some constructioner handy with tools, and therefore halve the cost of building. Perhaps in the fall he can make a trade by promising planting assistance come spring.

To be realistic regarding the subject of brush weirs: they are rapidly losing their importance among the methods of catching sardines. About 60 per cent of today's herring fishing is done by seining, and the industry would never have grown up, according to one Maine expert, "had it depended solely on weirs as it did at the beginning of the century."

In the employment of seines you seek out the fish rather than waiting for them to come to you, as in the case of a stationary weir. Airplanes are used to sight the schools, and when the fish are spotted, the seining crews are alerted and the equipment is moved at once to the site, which generally is not too far offshore.

Two types of seines are utilized: stop seines and purse seines. The stop seine is stretched across a cove to restrict a mass exodus of the fish. Stop-seine twine is of such a dimension that it looks to the herring like an impregnable wall; he doesn't swim straight at it, but turns gracefully in the required direction. The stop seine is a long net of varying depth fitted at the top with floats, and its lower edge stretched onto the bottom with weights.

Once the cove is "stopped" the purse seine is brought together by tremendous physical strain — it must touch the bottom, and be constricted to complete the taking of the sardines. The purse seine is very like the stop seine except that on its lower edge are drawstrings in a greater way performing the containing function of an old-time piece of underwear. When laid around the school of fish, the purse string is gradually pulled together close to the bottom. The top of the net is hauled into the dories and soon all the fish are pursed together for pumping or bailing into the larger seine boat or sardine carrier.

A complete and up-to-date seining outfit will cost $20,000. It will consist of two large seine nets forty and fifty feet long, a large diesel-powered seine boat, and a supporting cast of three to four dories.

When fish were scarce in 1948, prices varied from $25 to $60 a hogshead. Since there are 17½ bushels to a hogshead, it is well understood why big packers have a solid concern for a fisherman's equipment.

Sometimes a catch of herring will be held in the seines or weir as long as forty-eight hours, while they complete their digestive processes, to get rid of the red feed. Meanwhile the fishermen stand by, hoping that no further plankton, the larva feed, will appear. Occasionally during such a vigil, a storm makes up; if it is of sufficient force to present the danger of losing the twine, the fish are released. Why take a chance with a seine worth perhaps $3000?

48

Powerful ease at Eastport.

The Reversing Falls at St. John, New Brunswick. Twice daily a thirty-foot tide forces the St. John River to turn back on itself. The passage is navigable for about an hour, but it is suggested that the local pilot's services be utilized. Glooscap, local Micmac god has received credit for this phenomenon.

Once the fish are transported on board the sardine carrier, huge bags of salt are ripped open and shoveled upon the new catch, now reposing in the hold. This action is called the pre-salt (there's another salting at the factory), to prevent deterioration before the boat reaches the cannery. Most sardine carriers are capable of transporting from 35 to 110 hogsheads of fish direct to the plant. Few boats, however, operate more than twelve hours from their home factory.

In the train of the sardine fleet there is frequently a "scale boat." About 1920, someone who had watched the plethora of shining scales glistening all over the

Approaching the Nova Scotia border, covered bridge near New Dorchester, New Brunswick.

Left: The Miracles of Moncton, an active metropolis named for a British general, is the site of two of the world's natural wonders. The Bore: the funnel-like shape of the Bay of Fundy forces an eighteen-mile tidal wave into the narrow mouth of the Pedicodiak River. Right: The Magnetic Hill. Probably an optical illusion but a sure 'nuff queer feeling when the car moves upgrade without power.

water must have hit upon an idea for their use. Since that time there has been a steady market for herring scales. These are processed into a pearl essence used to lacquer artificial pearls and buttons. Herring scale is also utilized for foam fire extinguishers and it has been applied to produce the finish on expensive automobiles.

When scale is being gathered, the "scaler," or "sucker," replaces the bailer. This is a large flexible tube, and it works on the same principle as does the little thing the dentist always puts into your mouth to collect the errant saliva. After the sucker has been submerged into the mass of herring, the power is started. Then the stream of water and fish starts upward. A guard over the mouth lets the herring in, yet it keeps out the hake and other fish. The fish are carried into a separator that abrases painlessly the scales from the sardines, depositing them through a fine screen on the stern of a smaller boat nearby, filling its buckets with silvery slop.

Up and down the coast there are big canneries: Rockland, Stonington, Belfast, McKinley, Southwest Harbor, Millbridge, Jonesport, Eastport, Lubec, etc. Maine sardine-packing plants have been operating for seventy-five consecutive years, with a current average annual production of three hundred and fifty million cans. There is one national can-manufacturing branch working very nearly the year round at Lubec for the sole purpose of supplying cans for the state's sardine industry. Still this is not enough. A Portland factory manufactures about one-third of the total.

In Lubec, a fat nubbin of land sticks out far enough to dispute any Eastport claim to being the most easterly point in the United States. The town sits on a high hill topped by a white church steeple like a candle on a birthday cake. The original steeple was twenty feet higher, but blew down in the Saxby Gale of 1866. Eastport and Lubec are closest of the American packing centers to the Passamaquoddy area, which from the beginning has been the source of the Bay of Fundy and Gulf of Maine sardine or small herring. The canning factories are moving westward, nonetheless. Since the catch holds good as far as Portland, there is practical wisdom in this migration: first, there are real transportation advantages of being near to the large metropolitan centers; secondly, the Bay of Fundy, close to Eastport and Lubec and having the greatest tidal range in the world, means difficulty in fishing the weirs. In the Rockland to Portland area, however, the weirs and scines, when full of herring, can be fished any time during the twenty-four hours.

Soon after he has been scooped from the sea, the sardine is reposing in oil and mustard or tomato sauce against the golden sides of his silvery can, and processing continues with all the parts he has left behind him. The heads, tails, and, in fact, all broken and rejected fish have been shoveled up to be treated in various forms as by-products. Dried and treated either for fertilizer or as feed for cattle, the mix, pound for pound, as fish meal represents five times as much protein as beef. Dried meal sells for $100 a ton and at five cents the pound.

The gourmet blesses the sardine for having few bones, which are softened to nothingness during the steaming process of the canneries. His naked head, his single dorsal fin, and an absence of "lateral-line" organs make him an uncomplicated little fish to eat. Despite the fact that he is desired by both cod and man, the herring — notwithstanding the relatively low spawning average — seems to have good chance for survival, at least the North Atlantic variety, *Clupea harengus*.

Farmer contemplates distant Charlottetown. Potatoes are one of the staples of the 160-mile island, "The Garden of the Gulf." Incidentally, this is the name of the Island's newspaper, which carries the subline, "Covers the Island like Dew."

VI

Pastoral Simplicity — That's Prince Edward Island

WHEN THE IRISH literary man speaks to erudite listeners of Æ, they click at once, although the two initials signify, it so happens, one George William Russell, who wrote, among other things, "The Nuts of Knowledge." The Master of the ES, contemporary of Albrecht Dürer, is sufficient to the Ph.D. mind in the art world. L.A. to the layman always means Los Angeles, and for the American public F.D.R. and R.F.D. have their distinct connotations. But P.E.I. can mean only one thing, especially to a Canadian — Prince Edward Island — although there are those who submit that the oft used letters should stand for "Peaceful, Enchanting Island." Prince Edward's was named for the boisterous Duke of Kent, Edward Augustus, well remembered for past performances at Halifax, Quebec, and other ports. He was important to history for being the father of Victoria Regina.

P.E.I. is a most sufficient spot, thank you, a perfect example of the word insular. The inhabitants, of which there are only about one hundred thousand throughout the island, speak of their excellent plane service as bringing the "foreign mail," yet the mainland of New Brunswick or Nova Scotia is only nine to thirty miles away, depending on which end of the Northumberland Strait you make crossing. When the native declares he is going "out west," he can be compared to the Floridian who plans traveling to "the west coast." You realize that neither will be leaving the reservation. For most Americans, their only picture of the Island was acquired at an early age via Lucy Maud Montgomery's *Anne of Green Gables*. This and subsequent books of the beloved unsophisticated miss with the red hair and the green eyes have sold in the millions. L. M. Montgomery was born in 1874, but her Anne volumes are still on the "out list" in American libraries, as you will discover if you attempt to ram down the throats of your children the reading that you enjoyed forty years ago. "Anne" represents the single greatest contributor to the Island's promotion. In an article on P.E.I., Mrs. Montgomery once explained her countrymen accordingly: "We are not hidebound or overly conservative but we do not rush madly after new fads and fashions just because they are new. We wait calmly until other parts have tried them out for us and then, if they have stood the test, we adopt them."

"The Island" — Minegor, as called by the Indians — lies in a semicircle of the Gulf of St. Lawrence. Prince Edward is but 150 miles long and from 4 to 40 miles wide, depending on where you cross. Ninety per cent flat, one handful of hills reaches 500 feet. It is the smallest province in the Dominion; in fact it would fit three hundred times into Quebec. Eighty-five per cent tillable, its land produces potatoes, turnips, berries, rye, oats, and hay. Its Malpeque oysters are as famous as any in the world. The monetary resources of the Island do not amount to much. At midcentury the entire island's income tax did not total quite three million dollars, whereas Quebec paid a tax tab of three hundred million. As there are few if any secondary industries on P.E.I., an Islander who cares not a fig for farming or fishing is quite likely to consider emigrating to the United States.

One of the most intriguing stories regarding P.E.I. fiscal adventures has foundation during the term of governorship of Charles Douglas Smith, 1813–24. Prince Edward merchants, finding themselves with an excess of Spanish coins, had been sending them to Halifax, thereby profiting by the most handsome rate of exchange prevalent. Smith pondered long on how to maintain the Spanish coins in circulation on the Island. Finally he called in all extant pieces and had a mechanic in Charlottetown punch out the centers; the inside area was to pass officially for a shilling and the outer rim was to be worth five shillings. The mutilated coins were declared illegal tender beyond the Island. The purpose of local distribution was apparently solved until suddenly they disappeared once more from circulation — that is, half of them did, the punched center pieces. It seems that a shrewd shopkeeper had discovered that the punch had included a trifle too much coin so that it contained nearly two shillings worth of metallic silver. Accordingly, the enterprising gentleman cornered the market and forwarded the centers to London to be melted down. The plan went awry, however, when the ship out of England foundered on its return voyage. "It is probable that the depths of the Atlantic hold the secret," says an old account.

But so much for the filthiness of lucre. The wampum days of Prince Edward Island revealed the same discovery pattern as the other Maritime Provinces and Quebec. Cartier came first, to be followed not too many years later by Champlain, as consistent a you-follow-me act as Gehrig shadowing Ruth in the Yankee's batting order.

Champlain, when he cruised along seventy years after Cartier, thought P.E.I. so beautiful that he named it for one of his favorite saints — Ile St. Jean. And of course there is record of Wolfe, who looked in briefly for fresh drinking water on his way to subdue Quebec. The Island received its quota of Nova Scotia's displaced Acadians, and Loyalists from sixteen American colonies. Highlanders were not long in coming from Scotland.

Cartier, the first white man, wrote enthusiastically of his discovery, recording that "the said lande is low and plaine and the fairest that may possibly be seen, full of the goodly meadows and trees" — trees which in many cases today have disappeared in favor of pastures and fields. In July of 1534 Cartier gave Malpeque Bay (near Cascumpeque) its name for a great number of canoes he saw there. Cartier also had his first eyewitness view of natives smoking tobacco. He writes: "They hang about their necks wrap'd in a little beaste skinne made like a bagge together with a hollow piece of stone or wood like a pipe. Then when they please they made a powder of it and put in one of the endes of the sayd cornetts or pipe, and laying a coil of fire upon it at the other ende they do sucke so long that they fill their bodys with smoake."

On the second of July, Cartier landed on what is now North Point; he called it Cap des Sauvages because of the great quantity of natives who, afraid to approach him, peeked out from behind trees. As Cartier, discouraged by the lack of success of his good-neighbor act, was putting off from shore, one of the bolder Indians ran out and made signs. Cartier hastened back but the now frightened red man retreated to cover. Cartier left a discovery token in the form of a steel knife wrapped in red flannel. He tied the souvenir to a stick, then departed to his boat.

Cartier was impressed with the red soil, which has intrigued visitors for subsequent decades. The scientists tell us that the explanation for the deep-brick dust loam comes from the disintegrated red sandstone coupled with no end of shales. But the Micmac Indians, whose descendants still live on the Island today, wearing the garb and following the manners of the white man, for years have employed a legend to explain the crimson-colored soil. According to the Micmacs, they believed that Thunder descended from the heavens in the form of a black bear to fish in the water. An Indian maiden gathering berries appeared at this inlet, not seeing the black bear, who was catching forty winks under a tree. Thunder was entranced with her beauty, and quickly changed himself into an Indian brave. Then he plucked a mayflower and tossed it in her direction: the Micmac procedure for asking the maiden to be his wife. Once she had nestled in his arms, they floated up to his heaven in the clouds. There she lived in all happiness, but being slightly on the gregarious side, she eventually fell in love with Morning Star. Thunder, in mad jealousy, sent her tumbling to earth. She crashed in the same sylvan inlet where she had first met him, her blood spattering over the rocks and turning them red.

One last comment of Cartier's regarding the bountiful soil: he tells us it was "full of peas and white and red gooseberries, strawberries, blackberries, wild grass like rye. . . . It only wants [he believed] for harbours." The harbors were there, Mr. Cartier. Not many, it is to be admitted. The shores are irregular with deep undulations. The rivers are frequent but small, in some cases curling almost all the way across the Island.

As a result of Cartier's voyage, P.E.I. was included in the undefined territory of New France. In 1663 it was granted as a feudal tenure to Sieur Doublet, a

Left: No hill in P.E.I. ascends more than 500 feet — very few of its acres are non-cultivatable. Right: The spud tragedian. Charlottetown in the distance.

French naval officer. After Utrecht, 1713, its agricultural possibilities lured large numbers of settlers from Cape Breton. Its ownership changed with the fortunes and tides of the many English-French treaties: taken by the British in 1745, it was restored by Aix-la-Chapelle; again it fell to the British after Louisburg. In 1758 the British, under Lord Rollo, conducted a partial evacuation, something like the expulsion of the Acadians in Nova Scotia three years before. Finally P.E.I. was officially ceded to the British in 1763 and became a separate government, breaking with Nova Scotia. Ten years later, in 1773, P.E.I. founded its own legislature — years ahead of our own Congress.

In London occurred a great grabbag lottery in 1767 for P.E.I. land, when certain favorites of the home government, mostly military men who had real or imagined claims against the crown, received sixty-seven lots of twenty thousand acres each — all prizes, no blanks. The only element of chance involved was the location of each gift of land. The P.E.I. register of 1830, looking back with sardonic allusion to the manner of parceling out estates, notes that "the pretty uninhabited island — was particularly rich in pensioned governors and ex-governors — nearly equally rich in pensioned widows." For one hundred and thirty years the results of this fabulous example of long term absentee ownership were not satisfactory. "Granters," said one account, "did not encourage fisheries or settle one person." Only a handful of proprietors actually settled their own land; and the absentee owners ever offered a stumbling block when an ambitious toiler of the soil desired to acquire a plot of ground he could call his own.

The results of the Civil War brought the Island's property problem into focus. Long memories were agitating to annex Canada for alleged violations of neutrality. It was obvious that the Canadian colonies, then separate from the Maritimes, were very much on the spot. It was decided to gather at Charlottetown, Prince Edward

56

Malpeque oysters are considered the finest.

Spreading sea moss which is used in blanc mange and other edible products.

Island, to do something about it, and quick. In the imposing Province Building, in a room which is now a national shrine and open to the public, the Canadian factions met in concert and sales-talked the possibilities of a federation. Three years later, this time at Quebec City, the Confederation was written into law for all except P.E.I., who, with typical insular independence, did not choose to go along. This, the historians say, was due to an unusual local patriotism and a momentarily prosperous self-sufficiency.

But pride leaves when poverty stalks. By 1873 an overextended P.E.I. had felt the pinch of finances, and she decided to join. At the same time the Island made a very constructive deal for herself on four counts: her national debts were to be paid by the Dominion; all disputed land from absentee property owners was to be sold to the settlers on reasonable terms; the current railroad obligation was to be taken on by the Dominion; and, lastly, the national government was to maintain a year-round ferry service from the mainland to the Island.

Regarding the all-this-and-heaven-too package, Lord Dufferin, Governor General for whom Dufferin Terrace in Quebec is named, commented with great restraint and evident wit, "The Islanders entered the Confederation gladly under the impression that the Dominion has been annexed to Prince Edward Island."

57

Tree-shaded Charlottetown, capital of the Island, and of course of the province, is not a "town" but the only city on P.E.I. Its population is about 16,000. The streets and the squares are generally named for the queen, King George, or their prince. Charlottetown is one of those places where all but one of the drugstores close on Wednesdays and each thoughtfully leaves a card in its window, announcing which of their number has the duty for that afternoon. Two-wheel carts full of coke or coal clobber through the city, but on the other hand Charlottetown has one of the most modern and comfortable brick hotels that will be your privilege to enjoy anywhere. The waterfront represents another perfect Canadian harbor, the confluence of three rivers (the Yorke, the Eliot, the Hillsborough) — so beautiful that when the French entered in 1733 they named it Port la Joie. On Sundays, when the city is booming with chimes, the citizens pour into the streets on their way to worship. Its inherent love of prohibition means that thirsty visitors have little opportunity to indulge their taste other than by means of liquor purchased in package stores.

In 1775 two American cruisers were stationed in P.E.I. waters on instructions to intercept troop or munition ships from England. Tiring of their nonproductive patrol, they sailed into Charlottetown harbor looking for trouble. They subdued the settlement, carried off the acting governor and two of his officers to New England. George Washington, who was at Cambridge at the time, on being acquainted with their act, was not amused. Instead of complimenting his countrymen, he had the three men set free, and delivered a firm protest. The acting governor, whose name was Challeck, acknowledged Washington's deed in a letter that is a pattern of exquisite English prose.

P.E.I. for years had its own divorce court, founded in 1837 and continued beyond 1871. But until 1945 all divorce cases on the Island had to be determined by the parliament of Canada. Years ago a man named Capell was directed by the court to contribute to his wife's support. He refused and was sent to prison. The husband enjoyed a financial position which would have allowed him to maintain both himself and his wife. But he preferred life imprisonment.

West of Charlottetown and south about forty miles is Summerside, the largest town of the five on the Island, its population around 5000. Its name means just what it says, for, in season, its glistening waters are spotted with pleasure sails. The most glamorous swimming, however, is on the long red beaches on the north side, where it is sometimes as warm as eighty degrees in summer, a phenomenon worth noting, considering the icy coastal waters of Maine to the south. Here, off Tracadie, Stanhope, and Cove Head, the breakers cream across the red sands toward the dunes of similar hue.

Although it is a proven fact that P.E.I. has less fog than its Maritime neighbors, the Island, also called the Garden of the Gulf, occasionally has its rain and deep clouds. Cloudy weather recalls another legend involving the Micmac's demigod, Glooscap. Glooscap especially hated rain. One day his enemy Big Beaver persuaded Gull and his brothers to shower the god with raindrops poured from huge birchbark buckets. The buckets were so heavy that they had to be rested on the clouds, and the clouds in turn couldn't stand the strain; they began to frown darkly and sink lower and lower. The legend is that whenever the clouds lower menacingly, Gull and his exasperating brothers are up there, ready to let go with their giant birch-bark buckets.

The Dominion and the Province have wisely established these lovely northwest

Red beaches on dark October day near the Anne of Green Gables country.

beach areas and dunes as national parks. Most all roads in P.E.I. are good. Occasionally the drive will pass along a clear lagoon that is divided from the sea by red sand hummocks and witch grass.

The national park development has extended to the locale of Anne of Green Gables and includes her old homestead at Cavendish. The white structure, not so far back from the sea, looks just the way as always described. Not far away is Anne's lake, Lover's Lane, and the Dryad's Bubble. The house and surrounding land is now part of a government-owned golf course, with good lodging accessible to all. Near the Gables is a solid gray monument to honor Mrs. Montgomery, who died in Toronto in 1942 and was later buried on her beloved Island. "Home must always be the loveliest spot in the world," Mrs. Montgomery once asserted, "no matter what fairer lands may lie under the alien stars."

Mrs. Montgomery loved her Island any month in the year. She speaks of an

August afternoon "when the blue haze is scarfing the harvest slopes, little winds whispering elfishly in the poplars, and the dancing splendor of red poppies . . ." In contrast, we enjoy the dour compliment to the month of November by a barrister and judge advocate writing in 1851. "Whatever you may have heard," Lawson, Esquire, says of P.E.I., "neither the severity of the winter nor the heat of summer is in the least to be feared. . . . There is nothing in the month of November to induce meditations of a suicidal nature."

The waters surrounding the Island are amazingly warm for a country so far north. As stated, in summer the bathing temperature off the red-sand beaches of the outer island sometimes reach a point as warm as Florida's. In winter, however, the sweep of salt waves in the Northumberland Strait between the Island and the New Brunswick and Nova Scotia mainlands are clogged with ice, which drifts from late December to early April. One of the great Prince Edward Island ferries, a five-thousand-ton streamlined steamer, is especially designed for sturdy ice breaking. This is the *Abgeweit,* called after the Indian name for the Island, Cradled in the Waves. It is capable of carrying an entire train of cars plus engine, a thousand people, and several automobiles.

In the old days before leviathan motorized ferries, winter crossings were particularly dramatic. Eighteen-foot open boats with double keels took from six to nine hours to make a trip less than an hour today. No matter how cold the weather, the passengers arrived on the other side dripping with perspiration — besides paying fare they had to row. Toil could be avoided entirely by paying double, but such deluxe passengers often had to get out and walk or else were involved with the elements such as blinding snowstorms which made holding to the course difficult. Baggage was free on board up to forty pounds per person; beyond this figure it cost three cents a pound, considerably less than the modern airlines charge for excess weight. There was a firm rule that liquor was not allowed. The crossing, through pyramids of broken ice, was considered dangerous enough without drunks. When the water showed clear, the sail was set. Sometimes between mammoth ice floes the boats ran into "lollies'" — slush ice that floats in globs several feet deep. Occasionally, while pushing the boat through one of the frozen areas, a crew member would drop through an air hole, to be saved by the leather straps extending from the boat. In January, P.E.I. weather averages sixteen degrees, rather rugged temperature for wet and frozen clothes in the Northumberland Strait.

We know that Alexander McDonald, later of Cincinnati, a millionaire partner of John D. Rockefeller, left P.E.I. in 1914. His rambling house has become a comfortable hotel. But those who remain in the Island seem rich in other than worldly possessions. There is a fine line between complacency and contentment, and man seems too contented here with his meager lot, if meager be the word, to cause much excitement good or bad. There are very few front page stories on P.E.I. Dorothy Duncan labors the point amusingly in her *Here's to Canada,* which, incidentally, is well worth acquiring. For the purposes of her book, she would appreciate it better if un-newsworthy, P.E.I. "would bite a dog." Books on P.E.I. are scanty. Your correspondent cannot too highly recommend, however, *Over on the Island,* by Helen Jean Champion and *Beautiful Canada,* by Vernon Quinn.

There was one little bit of excitement here in 1852, when authorities were

Left: Cove near the Wood Island ferry. Right: No Chartres, but twin-towered religion, P.E.I. style.

attempting to lay the last strands of the P.E.I. sector of the transatlantic cable at Port Borden. Just as the end was in sight, the vessel carrying the cable was having a bad time of it trying to get up to the shore. In fact it seemed as if the vessel would not be able to fetch the last long mile. A hurry call produced a yoke of oxen and some horses. These, with the assistance of a kedge anchor, made the cable secure around a post — a happy ending, for the cable was laid, and Frederick Newton Gisborne, cable protagonist, a direct descendant of Sir Isaac Newton, gets full credit. Wood Island ferry is forty miles below Charlottetown. Up at the same end of the Island, say fifty miles above, is Souris, a beach town of quaintness. Be not alarmed by the name which, of course, translates into *mice*. More than a hundred years ago, wood mice beat a path away from the doors of the settlement and into the forests and today the only reminiscence of the little animals is the name. Likewise the forests have retreated into the interior.

In almost any direction you may drive are fox farms, or at least there used to be, in the bonanza silver-fox days. The bottom fell out of the market a few years back because of a style change whereby women on Park Avenue gave up wearing furs that bulked large or took away from the slim-hipped look. In 1936, when the Island was shipping two million dollars worth of pelts, either silver fox or platinum, there were over 700 fur farmers. Over the years, hundreds of the live species have been sent to other countries for breeding purposes. There used to be a Dominion fox experimental farm near Summerside, which was open to the public and very likely still is.

Most Beautiful Island in the World claim could be hotly contested by Cape Breton Island, Nova Scotia. The Italian Cabots, employed by England, landed not far from the above site in 1497, wishfully thinking that they had reached Cathay. More important: the English now had a claim to the New World.

VII

Two Days Around Cape Breton

Run do not walk to the nearest island.
James Thurber

At Mulgrave, jumping-off place from Nova Scotia proper, one crosses the mile-wide Gut of Canso, that narrow yet deep and very navigable strip of water, to land with all four wheels on Cape Breton Island. This is one of the oldest names in American geography. Sebastian Cabot touched on its eastern tip in 1497, the period when Leonardo da Vinci was displaying Renaissance versatility, and most authorities believe that there were fishermen ahead of Cabot. The island extends so far east of the Dominion that it has been called the Long Wharf of Canada.

On arriving at the Port Hawkesbury shore, we may indeed be in another island world, but we are still in the Province of Nova Scotia. Cape Breton itself is 110 miles at its greatest length and eighty miles at its greatest width. No one is ever more than a few miles away from water. This is because of salmon rivers, an ever adjacent ocean and the Bras d'Or lakes, salt-water seas that almost cut the island in two. Our immediate land course is sixty miles upcountry, a slowly unwinding trail of glens, curves, and rills, to the town with the incredible name Whycocomagh, pronounced *whycogg'-uh-muh,* Indian name for "head of the waters." Following one upon the other are vistas of the mountain-and-water scenery, not grand or terrifying as yet, but a gentle indication of things to come, as the road runs along the Bras d'Or, one of the "arms of gold." At Whycocomagh an old pulpit is still to be seen on its outdoor site, standing in a field of wild flowers. Today the faithful of Whycocomagh worship in Gaelic, but in a kirk with a roof. The first part of the service has often been conducted in Gaelic and the second in English. For a long time no music was permitted.

The country has the look of the heathered Highlands. As for the people of the area, they have the same curious shyness and sincerity so evident in Scotland itself; most of their ancestors left Scotland during the Jacobite rebellion in the eighteenth century. It has been said that there is more Gaelic spoken today in Cape Breton than in the ancestral country.

Further curves and glimpses of spruce and blue water — every moment the expectation of seeing a deer; the final swing is to Baddeck. Abadak was the early name, Micmac Indian talk for "the place with an island nearby," which undoubtedly referred to Kidstone's Island, not far offshore and worth visiting for its splendid bathing beach.

63

Left: Baddeck, on a Bras d'Or lake of salt, where begins and ends the Cabot Trail.
Right: the corner of the cemetery at Middle River which contained not only cows
but the grave of the murdered youth.

All seems peaceful in Baddeck; even the tide scarcely recedes or advances.
The entrance of the Bras d'Or lakes does not receive the waters freely enough to
cause them to pile up as is the case in the Bay of Fundy. Nine out of ten visitors
to Baddeck swear that they will return, buy land, and retire. Few ever do. When
in Baddeck they forget how far away from home they are. Baddeck, while it has
sheltered some very important people — at least in summer — hasn't grown very
much. One writer points out that in 1793 it had ten white inhabitants, which is
ten more than Chicago had at the moment. The agaricaceous — mushroomlike —
nature of Chicago, however, swung its population to four millions in the same
period Baddeck was achieving its first-and-only one thousand inhabitants.

After its beauty, its very solitude was the appealing attribute to a certain few.
Alexander Graham Bell, inventor, born in Scotland, died in Baddeck an American
citizen, decided in 1885 that in Cape Breton there was a place where he could
escape hot summer weather. One of Baddeck's leading citizens — who has thwarted
the tensions of business to live here at Bute Arran the year around — tells of Dr.
Bell's amusement and astonishment on first discovering that his friend had already
in his house, of all things, a telephone. It was this same pillar of the community
(a lifelong authority on woolens and other handicrafts of the area) who put us
right regarding the nomenclature of his clansmen. "Scotch," he explained, "is
whiskey. Call us Scots or Scottish."

Bell immediately became enamored of the jewel-like village and countryside, an
exact replica of his native Scotland. Little by little he amassed land across the
lake. He never regretted his instantaneous fascination, nor did the Bell generations.
In 1952 there were fifty-two Bell descendants in summer residence at Baddeck.

Three miles outside of town on green heights overlooking miles of curving bays
and forests, Dr. and Mrs. Bell built a large harmonious estate, called it Beinn
Bhreagh (beautiful hill). Mrs. Bell identified herself with a local movement to
distribute the fine hooked rug and weaving work done in the village and nearby.
She went so far as to have an expert come up from Washington, where the Bells

64

resided in the winter, to supervise the project. Among other Cape Breton bene-factions, Dr. Bell instigated the breeding of multiple-nippled sheep and doubled the volume of sheep births. The wool from Cape Breton sheep, incidentally, is extremely fine. Dr. Bell founded the Aerial Experiment Association at Baddeck. The Honorable J. A. D. McCurdy, resident of Baddeck, who later became Lieutenant-Governor of the Province, as a young man flew the first plane to soar in the British Empire; the flight took place off the ice in Baddeck on the third of February 1909. George Kennan, authority on old-time Russia and uncle of a later ambassador to the Soviet, was a Baddeckite. Earl Grey, Lord Aberdeen, Lord Willington, and others were invited to see the early flights and enjoy the fishing streams. Gilbert Grosvenor, editor-publisher of the *National Geographic Magazine* (any edition of which, fifteen years old or current, alleviates those ghastly moments in the dentist's waiting room), married one of Bell's daughters and he too became a Baddeck summer resident. When the senior Bells died within a few months of each other, they were entombed atop their "beautiful hill." Local employees of the scientist built

The Margaree Valley, Parnassus of all salmon fishermen.

By one of the Lochs O'Law. Cape Breton, although pierced by the Bras d'Or lakes, still has its quota of fresh water.

his simple coffin of pine boards, carried it on their shoulders up to its resting place on the mountain grove; a handsome round boulder marks the spot and a sign implores tourists not to scatter their camera boxes, papers, lunches. The Bells and their friends did so much for Baddeck and the region that, by a special act of legislature, it became the only incorporated village in Nova Scotia where the right to take part in local government was granted to property owners who were not British subjects.

Baddeck, with the accent plumb on the second syllable, marks the unassuming beginning and end of the Cabot Trail. Eventually one cannot decide whether this celebrated road starting as a most modest country thoroughfare, is a trail or a boulevard. As it ascends to its more spectacular moments over the sea in the midst of the most beautiful mountainous coastal country as may be seen anywhere, there will be moments of concern about the brakes, water-cooling system, and so forth. No wonder the service stations at Baddeck, so many miles from Detroit, are well equipped.

By all means the clockwise approach to the Cabot Trail is preferable. Thus, the car holds to the inboard, the land side, for a majority of the curves. There is nothing particularly dangerous about the Trail, but when the setting sun is in the eyes, hanging to the outer edge of a curve and meeting a car at the same time make for a certain concentration at the wheel. Herewith, at Baddeck, it is recommended to start off via the Margaree Valley; then Cheticamp and the Cape Breton Highlands National Park to Ingonish and way stations.

The first hamlet is Middle River, so unobtrusive that it is hard to find; here the item of the murdered youth's gravestone may be of particular interest. None of the handful of residents have probably ever heard of the incident and know or care less where the grave may be found. Cows grazing in the little cemetery make the search more enticing; but on finding the well-worn oblate headstone, its letters reveal that justice more than a century ago was not done.

The story goes that the occupant of the grave, in the early days of this remote country, had been murdered at a dance by another youth following a tiff over a girl. The attacker was convicted and put in the local poky. While he was awaiting his fate, a band of his contemporaries — it sounds as if he had friends, and that there may have been extenuating circumstances — broke the flimsy bars of the jail and spirited the accused by canoe to the mainland. Thence he progressed to far-western Canada, where he prospered and became a most respected citizen. The family of the deceased never forgot, however; when the headstone was erected, it bore the legend that, according to the judgment of the jury, the victim had been wilfully murdered, and named the doer of the deed. The indictment set in cold marble made for so much local comment that the kin of the accused had to leave Cape Breton forever. Apparently the alleged murderer, in an era well before the advent of Canadian Mounted Police or Dr. Bell's long-distance telephone, forever enjoyed complete asylum.

This relatively gruesome incident does little to diminish an appreciation of the peaceful country unfolding along the road. Three little lakes encircled by mountains — almost miniature Lake Louises called the Lochs o' Law — bring the realization that Cape Breton also has its share of fresh water to complement the Bras D'or.

Cattle and horses, Kentucky bluegrass country without the white fences and paddocks. But here nature makes her own boundaries, casting a twisting brook between the green fields, a line of spruce, or an occasional bluff.

The country is opening up. The spruce are clinging to the hills but at a greater distance from the road. We are approaching the broad valley of the Margaree, where sheep are grazing along the edge of its streams, and it can be well understood why the experienced salmon fisherman has at some time in his life made a mental note to whip the pools of this valley. A few miles off the main drag is one of the many spots beloved by artists — Frizzleton, of the fascinating name. At Margaree Forks the Southwest Margaree joins the main Margaree River. I. Walton knows that salmon are nearby: in the Forks, Thornbush, Hut, and Long.

Left: After the green Margaree Valley the coast, a contrast of bold blue sea and red shale. Right: The glinting spire of the church at Cheticamp, landmark for fishermen and pride of the villager, who is generally a descendant of the French Acadians.

The river must meet the sea. And what a sea it is! The wide green pattern of the sloping valley has been supplanted by a sheer blue background of waves smashing against a red soil coastline and coves of rock shale. Prince Edward Island and the Northumberland Strait are well yonder to the west, at least a distance of eighty miles by water, and consequently P.E.I. is not remotely visible.

Moving along the open coast to Belle Côte, it is of interest that the inhabitants so far from Grand Pré are of Acadian descent and that they speak the French tongue. At Terre Noire, the dark texture of the soil explains the name, "black ground." Friars Head, next, is so-called because a huge boulder lying on its shores is supposed to bear resemblance to a monk or friar. Cheticamp is the first town of any size, about 3000 population; east of the town is the famed gypsum area, a fine commercial activity. The pride of the section is the lofty Catholic church, built of freestone from Cheticamp Island; its interior is supposed not to lack in any comparison with its exterior. Cheticamp is the font of hooked-rug-making in Cape Breton; much of its production moves through Baddeck for larger distribution elsewhere. Nova Scotian hooked rugs excel others anywhere in Canada, and Nova Scotian needlepoint — the colors and patterns — will rival, in the opinion of many, the effects achieved by Flemish tapestry.

Away from the coast, to the right and southerly, the supreme moment is approaching, the entrance to the Cape Breton Highlands National Park — the meat of the Cabot Trail. By this time the spruce have reappeared, deeper and in more profusion. Little River, an intense-blue stream, scampers over small white rocks as round and smooth as baseballs. Ahead the mountains are said to be not more than 1500 feet, though they seem much higher — perhaps their sheerness is what deceives. Coming up is the ride that Duncan Hines had said makes the Gaspé look like a flat road. A Nova Scotia tour book warns: "The hills are steep and careful driving is urged. Brakes and steering gear should be in first-class order and the chauffeur should be experienced." In retrospect, the "chauffeur" decides that the view and effects were worth it, and probably the curves and descents would not be considered particularly hazardous by a motorist from hilly West Virginia. The beauty of the first-level mountaintops that lie below, with the sea underneath, compensates for any dearth of guard rails. Ask the average Cape Bretoner if the road is risky; he will laugh with scorn.

Pleasant Bay, notched in the base of the hills, offers a lone gas tank and a welcome breather in the form of a few feet of flat land. Until 1927 this remote hamlet could be reached only by water or by a footpath around the ring of mountains above the village. Even today the road is closed in winter; the local mail carrier takes to his fine dog team and shouts the dizzy leagues between Pleasant Bay and Cheticamp.

A short distance on in the woods between mountains is another inviting stop. At the roadside to the right stands a celebrated Cape Breton landmark, the Lone Shieling, an exact replica of the type of shelter that is built in the Highlands of Scotland, where, during a snowstorm, the crofter may sleep at one end and his flock at the other.

Eastward ho! More curves up the slopes of North Mountain and down into the beautiful Sunrise Valley, the dazzling view of big Intervale, hills and more hills and the roll of vales; Cape North Mountain and Aspy Bay well beyond, with the North Aspy flowing through the valley. Two miles farther is a huge operation in gypsum and five miles farther, Cape North and Sugar Loaf Mountain, believed to be the original "Terra Vista" of John and Sebastian Cabot, for whom this brilliant road was named. At Aspy Bay in June 1497, the explorer and his son are supposed to have landed and claimed the new world for the king of England. It was a warm day in June, of sufficiently high temperature for the Venetians, these "Cabotos," to kid themselves that they had landed in tropical Cathay. When they arrived back in London, the king allowed them ten pounds — almost thirty dollars — for their trouble (perhaps they would have done better had they brought back savages), but England had a kind of claim to this part of the new hemisphere.

Going downgrade now. Coming into view is Neils Harbour — swordfishing grounds; on land, geologic treasure-trove of feldspar, mica, and pinkish quartz.

Here, at last, is Ingonish, where the French had a thriving hamlet in the sixteen hundreds and by 1740 fifty-four fishing vessels were sailing from here, but during the siege of Louisburg, Admiral Warren's frigates ravaged the settlement. In the year 1789 ten shillings each was offered for moose and caribou hides, but when nine thousand carcasses were found between Ingonish and Cape North, soldiery were sent out from Sydney to stop the slaughter.

The name Ingonish is supposed to be of Portuguese derivation, and the Portuguese may have had a fishing settlement here as early as 1521. The beach is wide and sandy; it was a favorite haunt of Alexander Graham Bell, who would come down from Baddeck in old clothes and camp out in a tent and perplex the native Ingonishers who couldn't understand why a famous man didn't dress the part. Ingonish has what the artists want — in fact, what any man with a soul and an eye covets. In the shadow of Cape Smoky, a vast headland bordering South Ingonish, is a fresh-water lake, and a carpet-like undulating golf course, a championship layout, whose eighteen holes are named in the best St. Andrews fashion — Killiecrankie, Tam O'Shanter, Hame Noo, Cuddy Lugs.

If you can afford it, South Ingonish offers one of those "spectaculars" in the Canadian hotel field such as appear at Lake Louise, Pictou, St. Andrews, Quebec, and the like, and how surprising to find these Taj Mahals so far from nowhere.

The Ingonish shores are littered with swordfishing craft. In these little boats, planks are laid across the bowsprit to form a tiny platform called a "pulpit," from which the standing fisherman casts his harpoon; the mast is equipped with rocker bars so that the lookout may steer effectively from topside when fish are sighted. The majority of Cape Breton's swordfish catch, however, is taken in the Glace Bay Sydney area.

Leaving Ingonish and climbing again — over Cape Smoky, actually a mountain — the trail is as beautiful as formerly but perhaps not quite as breathtaking. One passes through little fishing villages, hardly realizing which is which: Wreck Cove, Skir Dhu (meaning in Gaelic black rock), Briton Cove, and North Shore. Cape Dauphin is the promontory on the left for which the original Indian name meant "grandmother."

The administration building of the Highlands National Park is left to port. The road ceases ascending and descending. Forsaking the Cabot Trail momentarily, we are once more in the center of the Bras d'Or lakes. A speedy modern ferry, able to transport a handful of cars, purrs across the narrow waters at Englishtown. A sign on the slip pronounces the stipulations relative to priority crossings for Her Majesty's mail carriers, doctors, and others who have urgent business. Nearby an impressive tablet, the cairn type so popular in Canada for national monuments, reads: "Saint Anne. Settled 1689 by Captain Charles Daniel and site of an early Jesuit Mission. Selected, 1773, as a naval base and one of the principal places in Isle Royale, named Fort Dauphin and strongly fortified. Its importance declined with the choice, 1719, of Louisburg as the capital." Declined seems the word for it, for the tour book lists today's population of Englishtown as 218, but there is nothing diminishing about the view, for this is the most fjord-like of all the Bras d'Or. Not far off in St. Ann Bay was caught a world-championship tuna, 977 pounds, and taken on a rod and line. Englishtown, which boasts one-half of one general store, has in its midst the ponderous grave of Cape Breton's giant, who died in 1863 at the early age of thirty-eight.

Angus McAskill lived the same number of years as Raphael and Thomas Wolfe and during his lifetime Angus was, in a physical way, just as famous. His seven-foot-nine-inch, four-hundred-pound frame came to be well known in the United States and Europe, and it is said that he was a fine-looking man, religious and upright to a degree, and that his knowledge of the Bible was extensive. He was born in 1825 in the Hebrides islands of Scotland and, typical of most muscle-binders, he was a sickly child. His father, who was only five-foot-nine, took Angus, the bairn, by his six-year-old hand and led him on board the ship that was to take the family to Cape Breton to settle at St. Anns, Victoria County.

With the change to Canadian air, Angus grew to be gigantic — this can be proved by some of the clothing he left behind: one of his waistcoats can be buttoned easily around two full-grown men. In the Halifax museum a McAskill shoe measures seventeen and one-half inches. For some reason he seldom had to shave, but his voice boomed up from a larynx as deep and wide as an organ pipe. McAskill would take a glass on a rare occasion, and, when he did, he grasped in his twelve-inch-long hand a special wooden dish justly called a "tub," which held enough to put a two-bottle man under the table. He could farm with the best of them! A hot day when the plowing was too much for one of the horses, Angus took his place in harness beside the remaining nag and nearly wore his four-footed companion into the ground. He was not unwilling, despite the acute homesickness he felt for Cape Breton, to travel extensively for a New York promoter in joint billing with the midget Tom Thumb. In one of their acts Tom would dance on McAskill's palm, hide in his pocket, or throw mock fisticuffs at his partner. Queen Victoria invited McAskill to Windsor Castle, chatted for two hours, and presented him with a pair of gold rings. Hard put for some demonstration of his strength adequate for Her Majesty, Angus walked up and down the royal drawing room, cutting the carpet to pulp under his great heels. Whether Victoria was amused is not recorded. By the time he returned to St. Anns, he had a snug fortune; he built a small store and "stocked it well." Though liquor was not his line, he was not averse to standing the customers to one on the house when the thought moved him.

The end came unexpectedly to McAskill. After a week's session with what was called brain fever, he "expired as a child falls into a peaceful sleep"; his coffin was large enough to float three men across St. Anns Bay. Our friend in the service

71

Into the Cabot Trail — high road but a wide one.

station at Baddeck who somehow came in possession of the quaint original head-stone on McAskill's grave, displays it in the garage window. Why the authorities replaced it for one larger but not nearly as artistic (at Englishtown) is a fair question.

St. Anns (this corner of the bay named by the Jesuit fathers for Queen Anne of Austria) may not be able to claim McAskill's burial place, but it is the site of St. Anns, a low wooden structure euphemistically called a "college," where courses in weaving are taught. Most astounding among the offerings of the curriculum is the opportunity to elect Gaelic. Summer visitors may sit in on classes. On the opening day of the college, which was dedicated in 1939 by the premier of Nova Scotia, the twenty students, ranging in age from sixteen to sixty, greeted him with shouts of "Maduinn mhath dhuibh a mhaighistir!" (Good morning, teacher!)

There is also a collection of McAskill relics, and, if you like that sort of thing,

72

Cabot Trail gives way to the Gaspé in length but not in precipitousness.

old farming implements and household utensils. Such were used by the flock of the apocryphal Norman McLeod, who was part highland chieftain, preacher, teacher, and leader of transocean pilgrimages, and was one of thousands of Scotsmen evicted during the Jacobite rebellion. After landing near Pictou on the north shore of the mainland of Nova Scotia, he preached and prayed so earnestly that he persuaded his following, "Normanites," to pick up ship and proceed farther for, of all places, Ohio. Storms, however, forced the pilgrimage in reverse and to a landing at St. Ann Bay, only a hundred miles away.

McLeod was not ordained until middle age, yet at St. Anns he went on with his teaching and preaching with all the authority of an elder of a kirk in Scotland. His hatred of earthly vanities was enough to influence the women of the clans to replace their colorful bonnets with kerchiefs and hurl their hair crimpers and meager trinkets into the bay. He even broke a lance or two for total abstinence in the clans — a tall and quixotic order.

McLeod had reached the age of seventy-two and that summer the potato crop had failed; he considered this an omen that the community should seek other pastures — this time to Australia whence McLeod's son had sent alluring reports. Straightway St. Anns carpenters built a five-hundred-ton bark that carried the minister and his family and thirty of his people halfway round the world. Thirty-eight clans were to be represented in the hegiras that followed during the next decade.

Disappointed with Australia, McLeod and followers removed two years later to New Zealand, where the government gave them several thousand acres north of Auckland. Their descendants today form a highly desirable element of the dominion down under. When the Reverend McLeod died at eighty-seven years, a monument was erected to his honor at Waipu.

Today in the St. Anns district there are plenty of lairds named for the great chieftain. McLeod's descendants and the kin of other clans gather in midsummer at St. Anns for the celebration of the famous Gaelic Mod. Participants come from Scotland, the United States, and distant points of Canada; a prize is given for the highest clan registration. Lads and lassies in competition sing songs and deliver poems — some original — and mostly in Gaelic. Bagpipes skirl and violins play, sporrans jangle, tartans and bonnets toss to the complex figures of the Highland flings and traditional sword dances. No midway, no dusty sideshows, no litter of lunch wrappings and banana peels. When clans have registered and elected their chieftain for the forthcoming year, the premier of Nova Scotia and other distinguished personages deliver speeches, sometimes in Gaelic, sometimes in English. The presiding voice at each Mod (pronounced *maud*) has been flown from his ancestral seat in Scotland at the invitation and expense of his Cape Breton clansmen. In fact no Mod has ever been held without the presence of the chief of the particular clan which that year is gathering in reunion. Visualize a college twenty-fifth reunion without its chief marshal! The MacCleod, the McNeil, or the MacClean recalls in glowing terms the loyalty, the quality and quantity of his clan. The distinguished ceremony of the Mod lasts a full week.

Most of this is described in Arthur Walworth's *Cape Breton: Isle of Romance.* Reflecting that Highlanders have always been considerable among men, Walworth quotes Dr. Johnson as saying in the Hebrides: "Civility seems part of the natural

Ingonish and some of its many swordfish boats, bow pulpits for the harpooner and topside gear to aid steering while conning for fish.

character of Highlanders. Every chieftain is a monarch, and politeness, the natural product of royal government, is diffused from the laird through the whole clan."

Our particular Cape Breton journey, meager in mileage compared to the wanderings of McLeod, has now completed very nearly a full circle since leaving Baddeck. The adjacent Ross Ferry, however, leads away from Baddeck across another narrow arm of the Bras d'Or and offers egress to Sydney and Louisburg.

Turning our backs on perhaps the loveliest country of the entire tour, the trek is again due east toward Little Bras d'Or to traverse the island of Boularderie, named in honor of Chevalier de Boularderie and granted to him for distinguished service in the defense of Port Royal (Annapolis Royal) in 1707. Not so fortunate thirty-eight years later, both he and his son were taken prisoner at the siege of Louisburg. The island, hardly recognizable as such, thirty by six miles, represents the best soil in Cape Breton.

Within the Sydney area, what's under the soil and sea commands the show. The coal-mining atmosphere may defeat Cape Breton's valid claim to be the Most Beautiful Island in the World, but the operation is of tremendous importance to Canada. Coal was first dug here in the eighteenth century to supply the fortress of Louisburg, but later, empire-thinking restrained Cape Breton mining for many years lest it conflict with the production of the collieries in England. Today Glace Bay, up the road thirteen miles, so-called because of the frozen condition of the harbor in winter, is the largest "town" in all Canada (6000 acres), with its population skirting thirty thousand. Its number two colliery has been the greatest producer in the Dominion. Most of its mining activity extends miles under the ocean. Close by at Port Morien, known as Cow Bay, a tablet announces that here are the remains of Canada's first coal-mining operation.

Hundreds upon hundreds of swordfish are brought into Glace Bay during August, September, and early October, and the tuna is off there too. From Glace Bay, steamers leave with regularity for Newfoundland seventy miles away.

As the road labors through North Sydney we suffer nostalgia for the landscape of the Cabot Trail, for this section begins to resemble a junior Pittsburgh. Sydney has a population upwards of thirty thousand. Presumably fortunes have been made here, and the original owners enjoy a fine absentee existence in surroundings beyond the tropical seas; but those who stay at home can boast an important farm market and a fine harbor, in wartime a rendezvous point for great convoys. We are told that there are fine parks within the city, and in the business area an inscription reads: "Cape Breton-Newfoundland cable. This tablet commemorates the successful laying in 1856 of a submarine telegraph cable between Cape Breton and Newfoundland as a part of a plan for speedier ocean communication, out of which later developed the Atlantic cable." Marconi, assisted by a grant from the Canadian government, worked in a house not many miles away.

Sydney, founded in 1785, some time after Louisburg, was first known as Spanish Bay and then named by the first governor of Cape Breton for the home secretary,

Left: The wheel again, perhaps the symbol of this trip — here on an Ingonish beach road at dawn. Right: Some miles beyond Ingonish father and sons throw together boat which will be sledded down to the sea come winter.

Leaving the Cabot Trail. Again the Bras d'Or lakes, an ocean within mountains.

Lord Sydney. Its first settlers were Loyalists from New York State, under the leadership of Abraham Cuyler, a former mayor of Albany, and in addition, Scottish Highland immigrants came over in 1802. The old Anglican church, fourth in the Dominion, has a chair from Nelson's flagship *Victory* donated by the wardroom officers on a visit to the port. Sydney operates what the guidebook calls the largest "self-contained" steel plant in America, complete with all the fixings — coke, pig iron, steel rails. The world-renowned Mackie process for hardening steel was evolved here. Nearer Great Britain than any other port on the mainland, Sydney is almost 600 miles closer than New York to Rio de Janeiro. The map of the two continents reveals that northeast South America bulges eastward and directly under Cape Breton. Joseph Barres, around 1800, was passionately interested in geodetic survey, but he came ashore long enough — and, after all, his trade was engineering — to build Sydney.

Considering the subject of engineering, twenty-three miles due east, most easterly point Down East, lie the relics of the once great citadel of Louisburg, originally a wonder defense. Its harbor of the same name opens on the broad Atlantic, and today the town numbers only about a thousand people who pursue the cod, the activity that originally brought European fishermen. Four centuries later, Gorton-Pew, American company of codfish cakes fame, constructed a modern processing plant.

The first lighthouse on the Cape Breton coast was erected here in 1751, and, incidentally, it was the first concrete building in America. Coal was burned in an iron pan set on a tripod, but the beacon could be seen only six leagues. An oil lantern was put up in 1736, but it was shot away during the second siege of Louisburg.

The sieges were thirteen years apart — the first began in 1745. A glistening little museum serves as the keystone for 300 acres purchased in 1920 for the Louisburg National Historic Park. Streets have been exposed and walls reopened, but on the whole the historic story of Louisburg seems more exciting than the ruins.

The Treaty of Utrecht, 1713, felt from Castine to Grand Pré, precipitated Louisburg. England had received Acadia proper, New Brunswick, and parts of Quebec and Maine. France retained Cape Breton, then known as Ile Royale, and Prince Edward Island, formerly the Ile St. Jean. The French realized that Cape Breton, early landfall from England, would represent a delectable plum and that a large effort would be required to hold it. Four years after the treaty, construction began under the architect-engineer, the Marquis Sébastien de Vauban, renovator of the Paris Bastille; it was to be a twenty-year job, and a bill to total twenty-four million dollars. The walls rose thirty feet high and ten feet thick; on the outside was a ditch eighty feet wide with bogs beyond. One French officer boasted that the fortress was so impenetrable that it could be held by an army of women. The king of France, for whom it was named, donated a huge bell (that later ended up in Portsmouth, New Hampshire, a souvenir of a Yankee raid). Louis XIV also had a medal struck off to commemorate the official founding of the city; later, in checking some of the bills, he asked if the streets were paved with gold. The fact that there were thirteen streets in the plan intrigued invading New Englanders, who considered the number an omen. With the completion of the city, merchants and fishermen began to prosper and nearby Acadian farmers grew rich. Those inside the windswept, and often fogbound, fortress led as gay and sophisticated an existence as possible; during the long cold winters there were giddy balls and routs.

The French forces at Louisburg occasionally threw their weight around. Commander Duquesne had sent a force against Canso and Annapolis Royal in 1744. Consequently, the impression grew among the British that, unless they had control of the whole Acadian coast, New England itself was in jeopardy — an opinion especially harbored by Governor Shirley of Massachusetts, a hard-bitten realist, so responsible for the expulsion of the Acadians.

On an evening in 1745, a fabulous armada rendezvoused off Canso, just beyond the old fort built by Nicolas Denys. The transports included a ragtail army of

4000 New Englanders — artisans, farmers, fishermen, and laborers — commanded by a merchant named Pepperrell and joined by a salty British fleet under the flag of Commodore Warren, summoned from Caribbean duty. Together they moved on to Louisburg, seventy miles up the coast.

An Indian, simulating drunkenness, waving aloft a rum bottle, was sent out to stagger to one of the outer bastions, a courageous piece of ham acting which proved unnecessary, for, to the amazement of the New England watchers, no resistance was forthcoming. Later, at other remote positions beyond the main fortress, a few guards were overpowered. These captured outer batteries, reinforced with an extra supply of cannon balls which the attackers had brought with them, now hurled defiance at the main fortress. Eventually the English perpetrated a trick possible in an era long before Marconi: they kept the French flags flying in the vessels they

78

Ruins of a twenty-million-dollar fortress at Louisburg. Looking toward the National Museum.

had captured in the harbor to decoy an unsuspecting French fleet sailing up the roadstead.

In recapitulating the forty-nine-day siege: the English sailors made out far better than the Army. The former got filthy rich commandeering shipping, while the troops contracted only a small raise in pay and plenty of fever and dysentery. After the fortress had been occupied, the military had little else to do but drink expensive rum; the combination of the thick sweet liquid, the harsh winter, plus a lack of replacements, put at least 800 New Englanders forever under Cape Breton soil.

To the disappointment of the English in New England, the Treaty of Aix-la-Chapelle in 1748 turned the fortress back to the French. Ten years later, however, the English were hammering away again — this time for keeps. Again an armada rallied outside Canso; 159 vessels under Admiral Boscawen, for whom the celebrated tavern at Lunenburg was named. Thirty-one-year-old Brigadier General Wolfe, later to reach immortality at Quebec, headed one of the brigades; the others were conducted by Brigadier General Whitcomb and Governor Lawrence of Nova Scotia. In supreme command was Lord Jeffrey Amherst, "Soldier of the King."

This time the French, augmented by their Indian allies, were on the alert. At first the turbulent surf made landings impossible, but after several days, although boats were overturned and many eighteenth-century commandos drowned, the British got through at "second Louisburg," despite the rain of shot and ball. For a while the French forces held on, but Wolfe, who seems to have been given all the tactical responsibility, maneuvered in brilliant fashion, silencing the Island battery despite the French attempt to block his progress by sinking seven ships in the channel. Six thousand became prisoners of war. The road to Quebec was now open.

The immediate result of the triumph was that the Island became a British possession and was annexed to Nova Scotia. Eventually the name Ile St. Jean was changed to Prince Edward Island and governed by Nova Scotia until 1769, when it became a separate province, the smallest in today's Dominion.

Louisburg was to be the embarkation point for Wolfe's expedition against Quebec a year later. Two years afterwards, when the British had gained both great fortresses, they determined to liquidate Louisburg lest it ever again be used against them. In 1760 under the direction of Commodore (later Admiral) Byron, grandfather of the poet, sappers and miners blasted and wrecked for six months, leaving rubble of what had taken a score of years to create. Today the blistered black cannon give indication of the hot fights that once enveloped the fortress; the old parade ground represents a handy spot to stretch the motorist's weary legs, to breathe the wealth of sea air, and watch the distant sheep nibbling grass on the ramparts.

The hard black road 100 miles back to Port Hawkesbury running along a broad Bras d'Or lake leads to the Gut of Canso and to the mainland of Nova Scotia, where we retrace our course, soon passing through Antigonish, site of St. Francis Xavier University, one of the finest institutions of learning in the Maritimes. In pronouncing Antigonish, the accent is on the last syllable (like Ingonish, Cape Breton, and Tignish, Prince Edward Island). To the Indians, who gave the town its name, Antigonish meant "the place where the branches were torn off the trees by bears gathering chestnuts."

Nova Scotia proper: late afternoon light on the Parrsboro shore. In 1621 King James of Scotland granted Acadia to Sir William Alexander and named it with a fine Latin flourish Nova Scotia (New Scotland). A coat of arms was granted, providing the unique flag of Nova Scotia. Standing on a plot of land within Edinburgh Castle, Scottish gentlemen were created "baronets of Nova Scotia."

VIII

Evangeline and Acadia

HENRY WADSWORTH LONGFELLOW contributed two poems to the literature of Acadia. One, scarcely remembered, pertained to the Baron de St. Castin; the second, in many respects a classic, was *Evangeline, A Tale of Acadie*. In neither instance did Longfellow visit the site of the piece.

The Evangeline story, laid at Grand Pré near Wolfville on the Minas Basin near the mouth of the Gaspereau River in Nova Scotia where the tides rise well over fifty feet, is probably Longfellow's best-known poem. Its first line, "This is the forest primeval," is just as familiar as "Gallia est omnis divisa in partes tres" of Caesar's Gallic Wars, or "Arma virumque cano," the opening of Virgil's Aeneid.

On the actual Grande Pré site, there was no forest primeval for miles around. As for the murmuring pines, there are few left today in either the lower Maritimes or in the coastal part of Maine; undoubtedly they would have been just as hard to find in 1755, the year of the expulsion of the Acadians. Longfellow likewise idealized the characters in his poem. "It is very possible," says Longfellow's brother, "that the poet painted in too soft colors the rude robustness which may have characterized the peasants of Grand Pré, as artists are apt to soften the features and clean the faces of the Italian peasant boys they put on their canvas. The picture of Acadian life, however, was but a part of his background. The scenery of Grand Pré he painted from books, having never visited the place, but it is sufficiently accurate for his purpose."

81

From Economy Mountain on the Parrsboro shore.

Approaching Truro — red-soil promontories and tidal effects.

Longfellow and Nathaniel Hawthorne had been members of the same class at Bowdoin College and had maintained a close friendship through the years. Both were living in Boston in the eighteen-thirties when Hawthorne, through Nova Scotia connections, came upon a word-of-mouth story of the tragic love story of Evangeline, daughter of the town's wealthiest man, and Gabriel, her muscular young lover, son of Basil the blacksmith. Hawthorne recorded the story in his notebook as follows: ". . . the story of a young couple in Acadia. . . . On their marriage day, all the men of the Province summoned to assemble in the church to hear a proclamation. When assembled, they were seized and shipped off to be distributed through New England — among them the new bridegroom. His bride set off in search of him, wandered about New England all her lifetime, and at last, when she was old, she found her bridegroom on his death-bed. The shock was so great that it killed her likewise." Later he read the memorandum to Longfellow, who commented, "It is the best illustration of faithfulness and constancy of woman that I have ever heard or read." Surprisingly Hawthorne seemed to have no designs on the story and relinquished his prior rights to Longfellow. The poet sat down to his research and among other writings leaned heavily on Thomas Haliburton's two-volume history of Nova Scotia. In 1847, the celebrated work, written in powerful hexameters, was submitted to Hawthorne, who rhapsodized, "I have read it with more pleasure than it would be decorous to express."

Longfellow in the beginning considered calling his heroine Celeste or Gabrielle. Most people will agree that the name Evangeline is more euphonious. Hollywood directors might differ. However, it is doubtful whether the role would have ever been suitable, say, for Rita Hayworth in flaming technicolor; and although it contains many of the elements of twentieth-century soap opera, its sad ending would have to be considerably altered for radio or TV consumption.

In ancient Arcadia in Greece (that central district of the Pelopynnesus, shut off from the coast on all sides by mountains), the inhabitants — shepherds and hunters — led a proverbially happy, natural life, worshiping Pan, Hermes, and Artemis. The French inhabitants of Acadia, Nova Scotia (most of whom could neither read

Beyond Amherst, an autumn day as clear as only the northwest wind can make it.

Tidal waters at Windsor. Nearby is the Halliburton Museum, whose 18th-century namesake created the whimsical literary character, Sam Slick.

nor write and most certainly had never heard of the Arcadians of centuries before), desired desperately to live a happy existence of their own, unmolested, and probably could have, had they had the wit to accept the simple ceremony of taking the oath of allegiance to the crown of England.

The area of Acadia has never been particularly well defined. It descends from the term given the maritime part of New France, or what are today the provinces of Nova Scotia, New Brunswick, Prince Edward Island, and sections of Quebec and Maine — roughly, the lands circumscribed by this book. The explorer Verrazzano called a part of the coast Acadia in 1524; the Micmac Indians used the term Acadie for "fertile land."

It was not until the coming of that important but relatively unsung personage of history, Pierre du Gast, Sieur de Monts, in the very active year of 1604, that any real attempt at settlement was made in Acadia. Cabot is supposed to have landed on Cape Breton in 1497 and Cartier on Prince Edward Island in 1534. The home base of De Monts and his cartographer-explorer, Samuel de Champlain, was always the Bay of Fundy and Port Royal, later to be named Annapolis Royal when the British took over. From here, Champlain made many trips as far away as Mount Desert Island, Castine, and even Cape Cod. Here was founded in 1636, the year of the birth of Harvard University, the first agricultural development by Europeans in what is present Canada. And now, at Acadia's core, continued one hundred and fifty years of shooting and strife, with the French, English, and Indians participating, bickering over a few miles of territory one way or another. Such protagonists as the La Tours and arch-rival D'Aulnay de Charnissy, and international fisherman Nicolas Denys were among those involved.

During the last seventy years of the seventeenth century, immigrants, to be known as "the Acadians," kept coming to these shores from their native Normandy. By 1700 there were almost 10,000 in the district, having settled at Annapolis Royal, on the Isthmus of Chignecto and in the Minas Basin. Their new homeland, with its enormous tides flooding the lowlands, was not unlike their native Europe. They took at once to building dikes and tilling the soil; they became closely knit and homogeneous, happy if left alone to worship in the Catholic religion. They became almost self-sufficient from the first moment that Pierre Martin planted the first apple seed in 1603. Young pear trees had also been brought with them from France and many of the aged willows seen today at Grand Pré were set in by the first Acadians. They lived in crude, thatched-roof huts and perhaps were not overclean. According to a historian, "They never made any merchantable butter, being used to set their milk in small noggins which were kept in such short order as to turn it thick and sour in a short time, of which they ate voraciously."

Parkman says in the first volume of his *Montcalm and Wolfe:*

> They were a simple and very ignorant peasantry, industrious and frugal till evil days came to discourage them; living aloof from the world with little of that spirit of adventure which an easy access to the vast fur-bearing interior had developed in their Canadian kindred; having few wants and those of the rudest; fishing a little, and hunting in winter, but chiefly employed in cultivating the meadows along the river Annapolis, or rich marshes reclaimed by dikes from the tides of the Bay of Fundy. The British Government left them entirely free of taxation. They made clothing of flax and wool of their own raising, hats of similar materials, and shoes or moccasins of moose and seal skin. They had cattle, sheep, hogs, and horses in abundance, and the Valley of the Annapolis, then as now, was known for the profusion and excellence of its apples.

> For drink they had cider or brewed spruce-beer.

> French officials describe their dwellings as wretched, wooden boxes, without ornaments or conveniences, and scarcely supplied with the most necessary furniture. Two or more families often occupied the same house; and their way of life, though simple and virtuous, was by no means remarkable for cleanliness. Such as it was, contentment reigned among them, undisturbed by what America calls progress.

> Marriages were early, and population grew apace.

If one seeks an unlucky date for the downward fall of the Acadians, 1713, the Treaty of Utrecht, serves as well as any. Then Acadia was ceded to Britain. It was agreed that the French settlers should be allowed to remain on their lands if they chose and worship in the Catholic faith; but if they desired to move out they would have to do so within the year. Few went on to other fields. Those remaining were asked to pledge an oath of allegiance to King George. Immediately there was trouble. The limited thinking of the Acadians refused to admit the possibility of pledging allegiance, despite the common knowledge that subjects go with ceded territory. Witness the ceding of Alsace and Lorraine in 1681, when no inhabitant was even asked to take an oath of allegiance but was commanded to fight for the French rulers without question.

From now on the Acadians (whose limited thinking indulged in complete obstinacy) were but pawns in almost half a century of international controversy and intrigue.

At first, harsh levies were applied to the French in Acadia. But these were palliated or lifted entirely when it became obvious that the collecting of same was almost more trouble than the sums involved. Phips, the Governor of Massachusetts and assaulter of Quebec, in his trips to Annapolis Royal was more than distressed by

Grand Pré — the bronze statue of the hard-luck girl, Evangeline, and she certainly looks it here.

the situation; he thought that it was definitely time to put the Acadians "on some footing."

From now on, the Acadians were caught well in the middle. The scheming priest Le Loutre, missionary to the Micmac Indians and vicar-general of Acadia, taking advantage of the ignorance of the people, gave them a one-way story by forecasting that to swear allegiance to England was to court eternal damnation. He stirred up the Micmacs to frequent raids on the British. Some of the younger Acadians added warpaint and feathers and went along on the massacres.

Meanwhile the French at Louisburg, that glamorous citadel on the Ile Royale (Cape Breton Island) did their best to manipulate the gullible Acadians into a nuisance front against the English.

Finally the English decided that once and for all they would have redress. A pair of outstanding instances of French opposition had been just too much for Governor Charles Lawrence of Nova Scotia and likewise for Governor Shirley of Massachusetts. It must be remembered that throughout this period, prior to the Revolution, New England was active in defense of the Crown and receiving protection therefrom.

First of all, not to be forgotten, was the massacre of Noble and his men: Arthur

Noble, colonel, and 470 New Englanders in search of a raiding French militia from Quebec had billeted themselves for the winter on the settlers at Grand Pré, having decided to wait until spring for a complete mop-up.

One February eve, having marched silently on snowshoes through a blizzard, the French militia attacked Noble and his men while they slept, killing sixty, including Noble and his brother, wounding sixty more, and capturing the rest. Coulon de Villiers, who led the forced march from Beaubassin, died later of his wounds. Undoubtedly the "passive" Acadians had been the informers. This one incident probably cooked their goose.

Eight years later a second nail was hammered into the coffin of the Acadians when their French superiors established the little fort Beauséjour. This is located on the New Brunswick border near the Missiquas River before crossing into Nova Scotia, an interesting museum for a visit today. The aroused English put two thousand New England men on the attack and soon the banner of the Fleur de Lis which had waved so defiantly above the fort was replaced by the British colors.

Still New England's Governor Shirley did not repose happily. He realized that the New England troops had enlisted for but one year and could not be kept in Acadia longer, and that the French would undoubtedly make a strong effort to recover their province perhaps as far south as Massachusetts. He felt that his only course was to replace Acadians with British subjects.

Meanwhile Lawrence's blood pressure was working up to an explosion, yet he, as governor of Nova Scotia, still would clear all action with the authorities at home. He again writes the Lords of Trade: "We are in hopes that the lenity shown to these people by indulging them in the free exercise of their religion and the quiet possession of their lands, would by degrees have gained their friendship and assurance, and weaned their affections from the French; but we are sorry to find that this lenity has had so little effect, and that they still hold the same conduct, furnishing our enemies with labor, provisions, and intelligence, and concealing their designs from us."

Then once more he sat back and gave the Acadians a chance to cultivate the affections of the English. The subject of the oath was brought up time and again. But by now the peasant "backs were up," so often the recourse of the rustic, who when pressured refuses to see what is best for him, even if a lack of compliance means destruction. They had picked the wrong pair to ignore in Lawrence of Nova Scotia and Shirley of Massachusetts. Besides, it was rather obvious that by playing dumb and calling themselves neutral the Acadians were little more than an enemy encamped in the heart of the province.

It was zero hour for the Acadians. Lawrence writes the following to the Lords of Trade: "I am determined to bring the inhabitants to a compliance or rid the province of such perfidious subjects."

Then a final refusal to taking of the oath at Annapolis. "Nothing," states the record of the council, "now remains to be considered but what measures should be taken to send the inhabitants away, and where they should be sent to."

John Winslow of Massachusetts, a descendant of one of the early governors of the Plymouth Colony, sailed from Boston with a shipload of New England volunteers to undertake for the last time the reduction of the difficult Acadians. Other officers were sent to Annapolis Royal and Windsor.

Murray secured 183 prisoners at Windsor. At Annapolis, a large group fled to the woods. Murray removed 1100 more from Windsor. There was a long waiting period for ships. By October, 1664 were sent from Annapolis and 1000 from Fort Cumberland. The whole parish of Cobequid escaped via Tatamagouche to the Isle of St. John. Altogether, however, a little over 6000 were deported, like so many sacks of flour. The rich meadowlands were swept bare beside the tidal rivers; homes of 6000 were burned to the ground, their cattle and grain forfeited to pay the cost of their deportation.

But we are particularly concerned with what happened to Evangeline. While Captain Murray was ensconced at Windsor, Winslow had encamped at Grand Pré. Neither had seen the other, but they indulged themselves correspondence in regard to the progress of their exporting of human souls, and to looking forward to shaking hands over a drink after the discharge of their unpleasant duty.

Winslow had done his task as humanely as possible. Taking his station at the church at Grand Pré he had the elders remove the sacred things for preserva-

88

By the "bending willows" it was in such a church at Grand Pré, of which this is a replica museum, that the Acadians were informed of the bad news.

Evangeline Beach, facing "the Look-Off." In the Minas Basin the tides will reach sixty feet.

tion. On September 5, in 1755, at three in the afternoon, 418 men and boys of the area were marshaled into the church, and instantly Winslow had his men surround the building. The day of reckoning had arrived. The decree was read. Through an interpreter, the definitive words of the proclamation began to penetrate their consciousness. According to Charles Hanson Towne, "for sheer brutality and hypocrisy it cannot be matched in history." Mr. Towne's lustrous book on Nova Scotia was published in 1923, some years before the edicts of Hitler and other totalitarian rulers. Grand Pré evacuation deportation led to no Buchenwald but it was tragic enough.

What happened to the Acadians after they became displaced persons? Considerable of their number were landed at Boston and were allowed to spread out on the Common but with certain restrictions in force. Others were shipped south, unhappy exiles for whom there was always the raised eyebrow, the obvious distrust. Those who were able to reach Maryland found more hospitality. Others got back to Nova Scotia after months and years and considerable walking through New England. There were those who found their old farm lands occupied by settlers from Connecticut; others came to rest in the coastal region between Digby and Yarmouth, St. Marys Bay, or as far as Cheticamp on the distant open shore of Cape Breton Island. When you see an occasional great cathedral in Nova Scotia, sheltering a little hamlet by the sea, usually the towers rise above the descendants of the Acadians.

But most fortunate of all were those who managed to end up in Louisiana, amid French people, where certain of the lands in Attapakas and Opelousas were assigned to them. At St. Martinville they were given a Spanish land-grant, 160 miles west of New Orleans, the locale for the closing stanzas of *Evangeline*. The house of Dean Louis Arcenaux, direct descendant of Louis Arcenaux, or Arsenault, who was the Gabriel of the poem, is now a shrine in Longfellow-Evangeline Park near the village.

"Evangeline was really Emmeline LaBiche," says Dean Arcenaux. "The pair actually came to Louisiana but the parallel ends there." Apparently the realist Louis (Gabriel) got there three years before Emmeline (Evangeline) and meanwhile, in a frontier country where wives were hard to come by, had married another girl. On her arrival the news was too much for Emmeline, who lost her mind. This version is also supported in *Acadian Reminiscences, The True Story of Evangeline* by Judge Felix Voorhies of St. Martinville, another direct descendant of "Gabriel."

The exiles found happy days in Louisiana and there has been an astonishing growth the length and breadth of the Acadian — or Cajun — country. St. Martinville, however, though rich in Acadiana, has stood virtually still. Those who are left of the original families point with questionable pride to the fact that there are more people in the cemetery than in the town. When Judge Voorhies died, his will directed with true Acadian sentiment that his coffin be cemented to that of his wife, which you may rest assured was done. André Olivier, curator of the little Acadian Museum at St. Martinville, tells that in his peaceful Teche country, where they call counties "parishes," French comes over the radio just as much as it does in Quebec, and that the majority preserve the old way of life even to the use of the horse and buggy along the green-bordered roads of the Bayou. Not until 1920 did wooden shoes disappear from daily life. Evangeline Oak still stands a few feet from the banks of the Teche; there is Evangeline's Grave, the Evangeline Volunteer Fire Department. Twenty miles away, at Lafayette, Louisiana, a regular stop for the airlines and the Southern Pacific Railroad, is the site of the well-known Evangeline Hotel.

How much should we weep for the Acadians who were forced out of Nova Scotia and away from its cold winters? By and large, those who managed to migrate to sunny Louisiana fell into happy, slothful days, were eventually blessed with a good living and a rich, "gumbo" existence. Perhaps they owe the British a vote of thanks.

Photographed in an autumn rain — apples and pears at a Kentville roadside stand. June offers the traditional appleblossom festival with the choosing of a "queen." Nova Scotia lost a vast German apple market in World War II.

Dudley J. Le Blanc, member of the Louisiana state senate and sometimes called the "King of Cajuns," has had no quarrel with his lot. He, too, was direct in line from Gabriel and has written a well-documented book, *The True Story of the Acadians.* Senator Le Blanc owned the sensationally successful patent medicine, Hadacol, advertised on billboards, mostly in the deepest south, by a rising sun over the challenging words, FOR A BETTER TOMORROW.

91

Events other than fishing have occupied the essentially English Halifax, which had the first public school in Canada, the first newspaper, the first printing press, the first Protestant church, the first dockyard and post office. The first hockey in America was played in Halifax on the first skating rink in the Dominion; Halifax had the first tennis court. Its history has been close to the achievements of Britain's army and navy. It was well named when called by Kipling, "The Warder of the North." Halifax, "Sailors' Town," is surrounded by the most picturesque fishing coves of the entire tour. It was cod like these (photographed at Indian Harbor) that first brought explorers, centuries ago, from the fish-eating Catholic countries of Europe.

IX

Halifax: Cornwallis, the Duke of Kent,
and the Explosion

THE BEST ADVICE for an all-over view of Halifax is to drive to the top of Citadel Hill. The city slopes down on a peninsula in the embrace of two glistening arms of water. The harbor is to the left and three miles away, the Northwest Arm to the right. From earliest days both harbors had their own advantages because they were long, deep and narrow at the mouth, and easy to defend by the method of stretching a chain across the entrance. The Northwest Arm today is devoted to parks and pleasure craft and is surrounded by pleasant houses.

The old Citadel or Fort George, a monument to the Duke of Kent, the royal engineer playboy, dates back to 1802. It was originally fortified by orders of the Duke of Wellington, who was on assignment in Canada after the Battle of Waterloo. The last important prisoner in the Citadel was Leon Trotsky. On top of the Citadel is the historic black ball which used to drop every day at noon so ships in the harbor could set their clocks. A sharp gun blast at twelve o'clock each day now serves equally well to pronounce the hour.

Speaking of clocks, below the Citadel stands the Old Clock Tower, erected by the Duke of Kent, who dearly loved timepieces and chronometers of all kinds.

From Citadel Hill, which was never attacked and yet acted as a buffer against the forces of the 1917 explosion. Looking upon the Old Clock Tower erected in 1802; beyond is the harbor, which shelters the shipping of all nations. Right: The ball was once dropped every noon to alert ship clocks in the harbor. Today the sharp blast of a gun seems to serve the same purpose.

Bar Harbor, Maine, versus Halifax Yacht Clubs. One of the latter has been permitted to use the prefix "Royal" since the days of the Duke of Kent. Right: Blown three and a half miles to this final resting place alongside the Northwest Arm is this part of the shank of an ammunition ship anchor. The ship collided with a French supply vessel in 1917.

The story goes that the stodgy old clock arrived from England just after the Duke, who had ordered it, had sailed for home, never to return to Halifax. No one knew how to assemble the intricate mechanism. It lay in a junk yard until a soldier came along who understood how to put the works together. Since that time the clock has run for 150 years, undisturbed except for one month when the numerals on the face, corroded by nature, were being refurbished.

Below the clock tower is the harbor itself. Perhaps a great ocean liner, one of more than thirty shipping lines that berth at Halifax, can be seen threading its way down to the open sea as small sailing craft relinquish their right of way at her warning. Wolfe's great armada lay on the same peaceful strip of water before departing for the expedition on Quebec. In World Wars I and II, several times the number of ships in convoy were spread constantly across the same port, which is two days nearer to Europe than New York is. Also within view is McNabs Island, where a Confederate cruiser, the *Tallahassee*, once escaped Union gunboats by maneuvering behind the island in waters that were considered unnavigable.

In the distance of the Dartmouth shore stand the refining tanks of Canadian oil companies, and planes hover over Shearwater base, named for a northern sea bird that skims close to the water in flight. Not all Halifax industry is visible at one glance, for the city refines sugar, makes chocolate candy and biscuits, and manufactures twine, paint, and varnishes.

Horace Sutton, in his *Footloose in Canada,* an essential for the traveler's book bag, presents an intriguing Halifax, old and new. Halifax, scarcely more than two hundred years old, is not a venerable city as cities go, but it was the first in British North America. The amenities were developed early. The original public gardens started as far back as 1753, only eight years after the first arrival. Today the Halifax Botanical Gardens, established in 1872, are full of fabulous trees, including Siberian, Japanese, Chinese, and other northerly species.

94

The city was established with a definite purpose in mind — English colonization as a check against the French position in the New World. On the longest day in the year in June 1749, a fleet of thirteen transports bearing 2576 English colonists and escorted by a sloop-of-war reached Chebucto harbor. The leader of the expedition was the Honorable Edward Cornwallis, twin brother of the gay Archbishop of Canterbury and uncle of Lord Cornwallis who, as every American schoolchild knows, surrendered to George Washington at Yorktown. The new post in America was named Halifax to compliment the First Lord of Trade, George Dunk Montague, Earl of Halifax. The Earl's title merits a moment of discussion. It derives from the city in Yorkshire, England, which in turn achieved its name from the fact that someone of virulent nature once had murdered a beautiful blond girl and had hung her head from a tree in the village. Halifax means "holy hair."

On the subject of hair lifted forcibly, the first Halifax settlers, a few of them,

95

Portuguese Cove, a few miles beyond Halifax's Northwest Arm, provides both the practical and the picturesque.

learned what an Indian massacre could be for the French paid a fixed fee for English scalps. But despite these French-instigated warrior raids, despite the infectious diseases which killed so many in a summer unbelievably hot for a northern country, the settlement with its lines of huts, stockades, and blockhouses survived. Some of the people lived on the transports in the harbor; sawmills were erected on the Dartmouth shore. A wharf was built for ships up to 2000 tons and a road was cut through to Minas.

It must be remembered that the blood stream of the expedition had been fed by the British Parliament. The British Government appropriated forty thousand pounds for initial expenses and also agreed to feed the emigrants for one year and supply arms for defense and farming equipment. Cornwallis drove himself into an early grave trying to get accomplishment out of the "English rabble," whom he called "generally tumultous, refractory, full of discontent and murmurings." He enjoyed a small measure of relaxation and contrast to his drab surroundings, withal to the dismay of his pious colonists, by an occasional barge trip up the harbor with his beautiful maroon mistress. Nonetheless, the settlement emerged as an effective garrison, at least a counterpoise to the French fortress of Louisburg, proudly rooted on the most easterly point of Cape Breton Island.

One of the new government's first concerns was to erect a wooden church capable of holding nine hundred worshippers. This was St. Paul's, which is still standing, the oldest Protestant church in Canada. During the explosion of 1917 a piece of flying debris broke through a church window cutting out an exact likeness of the profile of the rector. The congregation insisted that the miracle be preserved in a space in the church. The first organ used in St. Paul's was taken from a Spanish prize brought into Halifax harbor.

In 1752 formal peace was made with the Indians. The first press in British North America produced the first newspaper, the *Halifax Gazette*. Then came a long line of "firsts." The Royal Dockyard is marked by a tablet reading: "here James Cooke, the famous navigator and discoverer, was stationed in 1759 and superintended the erection of the first buildings." Another proclaims: "Shannon and Chesapeak. In honour of Captain Philip B. V. Broke and officers and crew of the H.M.S. *Shannon,* who gained a glorious victory over the United States frigate, *Chesapeak* off Boston harbor, June 1, 1813. The Shannon brought her prize to Halifax harbor on the 6th June." The Dalhousie Tablet explains how the celebrated university was started from custom duties raised at Castine during the British occupation of the War of 1812.

Whereas Cornwallis was the pioneer of Halifax, it was the Duke of Kent who gave it its personality. The Duke, a cosmopolite, had lived all over Europe, and in Canada for a time above Montmorency Falls (outside Quebec) in a distinguished white mansion; and he improved the Citadel defenses. He had governed Gibraltar until his attempt to effect prohibition of wine and spirits among the soldiery had produced a rebellion, an attitude which seems odd, coming from a *bon vivant* who has been described as a portly, energetic gentleman wearing a three-cornered hat and sporting a red waistcoat. His royal father, by cutting him off in youth with an allowance of but a guinea and a half a week, made sure that he would always be in debt.

When he arrived in Halifax town, it was filled with colonists who had been too long away from the sophistication of late eighteenth- and early nineteenth-century English taste. The Duke set out to embellish the drab surroundings. Halifax, a military town from its first day, with a hill crying for a bastion, was made to order for the Duke, who loved fortifications as much, if not more, than a pretty ankle. Up went the citadel and related fortifications. Before the Duke had finished with Halifax it became a swirling port of Georgian folly. West Indian seamen in outlandish garb walked the streets, beautiful women wearing absurd hoop skirts rode in open carriages, tilted their parasols, and tossed their lace handkerchiefs at dandies in high hats.

Vendors sold hard-boiled gulls' eggs, lobsters, cakes, and apples. Indians purveyed their usual handicraft. For his beautiful sweetheart from Martinique the Duke built a fabulous residence, where he gave balls and garden parties. It was surrounded by grottoes and arbors and had a lily pond cut into the shape of a heart. All that remains of the house is the round music room, which is open to the visiting public and can be seen close by the road coming into town from the Bedford side.

Shapes and shadows at Portuguese Cove. The ramps serve in lieu of more facile landing spots.

Left: The entrance to Portuguese Cove. Right: The "Novey" boat — through a frame of glass-ball floats and nets.

Eventually Kent returned to England, heeding the call of his country for a queen and an heir. He married the princess Saxe-Coburg and fathered Victoria, who as queen was in later life to pay his bills. Meanwhile, his exotic Julie was cast aside like yesterday's two-dollar ticket on the Derby at Epsom. The story is, of course, that Julie pined away in a Nova Scotia convent and soon died.

Today Halifax, often called the "sailors' town," is still a city of forts, naval happenings, red-coated soldiers. Most of the Canadian Navy is based here; Her Majesty's ship *Stadacona* is a huge naval receiving station complete with parade grounds and quarters for the officers and families and enlisted men. The war population of Halifax soars from a normal eighty thousand to a third as many again and such overcrowding with military personnel has produced its problems. For example, when, in 1945, the happy news of VE day was announced, the naval forces were suddenly given their liberty. Waterfront civilian rabble were precipitated into a flood of destruction that included the sacking of government liquor stores. Restaurants, movie halls, and other places where service men had not always been too welcome now felt the aroused impact of the extroverted mariners. Damage ran into millions.

The worst effect of a war that Halifax ever felt came on December 6, 1917. A Norwegian vessel, the *Imo,* loaded with supplies for starving Belgians, was rammed by the French ship *Mont Blanc* carrying a bursting load of TNT. For a few moments the ammunition ship reacted like a slow-burning fuse, a ghastly blue flame hovering over the hull. Then the blast let go. Nearly two thousand people were killed. Of those who rushed to the windows after the initial roar, another two thousand lost their eyesight when the devastating vacuum created by the blast sucked the air against the windows, shattering them in splinters. One doctor worked forty-eight hours without rest, just removing shattered eyes. Six thousand were wounded and ten thousand made homeless. To add to the diabolical com-

Peggy's Cove where a fissure of sea water extends up into the granite. Mr. Artist or Photographer, stand by. Your subject matter will compose itself — a dog, an old fisherman, a dory full of nets, and, always stationary, the adjacent lighthouse.

plications of the following night, a snowstorm blocked all rescue operations, including the relief trains coming from Boston and Portland. Ten blocks of houses were given by New Englanders to the stricken people of Halifax.

It is hard to believe that no traces of the physical damage to property remain in Halifax today.

Lunenburg schooners. One such as these, the *Bluenose,* a freak of speed, outfooted all vessels that fished the Grand Banks.

X

Lunenburg and the *Bluenose*

> The Captain never blew his nose
> Because he knew his nose was blue.

IT HAS BEEN SHOWN how the European Lübeck, one of the chief cities of the Hanseatic League — that loose but effective commercial federation of North German towns of the Middle Ages — had been the namesake of Lubec, Maine. Lübeck, Germany, has today a population of 225,000; Lubec, Maine, only about 4000. It may be not irrelevant to make the point that whereas the herring began to leave Lübeck in 1425, thereafter to disappear forever, on the other hand there seems to be plenty of herring, or sardine, in the Lubec waters.

While in the mood of comparison, we have another instance of naming another stern North American town for one in Germany. This occurs in the case of Lunenburg, Nova Scotia, which was named for Lüneburg, Germany. Like the German Lübeck, the German Lüneburg was a member, though in a lesser degree, of the Hanseatic League.

Lunenburg, 60 miles south of Halifax, started life as an agricultural section. Today, however, it is known best for its shipping and for having the most famous, or at least the most romantic, fishing fleet in the world; surely the most beautiful vessels.

Our Canadian Lunenburg had its start in 1753, when Colonel Charles Lawrence, later governor of the Province, sailed down from Halifax on a June day with 500

101

Left: Lunenburg — a happy town when life and play revolve around the schooners fitting out for the pursuit of the cod. Right: These dories will see duty from dawn to dark at the fishing grounds.

Barrels of alewives on the Lunenburg docks.

settlers. The majority were foreign Protestants: German, French, and Swiss who had first landed at overcrowded Halifax. Arriving now in positive Indian country, they first erected a blockhouse, which immediately saw action. There were some bitter skirmishes and scalpings, but before too long the Indian name for the place, Merlinguesch, was supplanted by the settlers' title — Lunenburg.

Not in a single generation did they become seafaring people. But they were faced with the problem of transporting their produce to market at Halifax. It had to go by sea, and boats had to be "fast and able." Also, the great fishing grounds of the cod, Labrador and New Foundland, were, relatively speaking, just off the coast. A few New Englanders settled there in 1768 and they taught the Lunenburgers how to build ships and perhaps how to sail them.

This "Captain Courageous" town, which sends its racy 130-foot black "cod-lining" schooners to the Grand Banks in a day and a night, is unique in comparison with the "States," where only one such schooner is still catching cod by the hand-line method.

A few miles from Lunenburg is the Blue Rocks, a small fishing cove, important to the artists, and one of the most remarkable painters of all times lives at Lunenburg, Earl Bailey. Born without arms and legs, he holds his brushes in his mouth. His technique is just as sure and solid, his pictures as colorful and vital as anyone could ask for.

Harking back to old Lunenburg: a year after the settlers had arrived, they built St. John's, the second oldest church in Down East America. It will seat a thousand people, and since it had the eighteenth-century blessing of the Royal Foundation, its communion vessels were presented by King George III, and the members of the choir are entitled to wear the official scarlet cassocks. The Queen Anne pewter chalice, used in 1754, can still be seen and the church peal of bells is heard for miles around.

Lunenburgers are long on pageantry and their most impressive ceremony is the rites called the Role of the Dead. According to Clara Dennis, in *More About Nova Scotia,* "The whole assembly forms in ranks of captains and crews of fishing vessels, heads and employees of the outfitting firms, the fishing firms, clergymen of the various churches, mayor and members of the town council and, last, that indescribably pathetic group, — the relatives and friends of the men lost, with the town band and the church choir at their head, — they slowly march down the long street and onto one of the wharves." Four boy scouts carry a fish barrow full of floral pieces. The first one is in the form of an anchor that the mayor reverently drops into the sea, the town's tribute to the lost fishermen. One by one the garlands are

On the go again. Such sights as these on the Shore Road near Shelburne, once famous as the seat of Loyalists. Oxen will be seen again in the French country from Yarmouth to Digby.

cast over the side, the flowers break away and float with the outgoing tide; the vast grave of the deceased is now festooned. The band plays the fisherman hymn known to all sailormen everywhere.

> Eternal Father! strong to save,
> Whose arm hath bound the restless wave,
> Who bidd'st the mighty ocean deep
> Its own appointed limits keep:
>   O hear us when we cry to thee
>   For those in peril on the sea.

The back harbor that shelters the lean Lunenburg schooners appears to be as placid a river as one could ever see. Whatever the dangers and tension on the Banks, Lunenburg itself seems to be a happy town. While the sleek black schooners are being fitted out for the deep sea, children slide down the tarpaulins covering the all-important fishing dories stacked near the pier, or else swing on the lower shrouds and rigging of the ships themselves. Any one of the genial-looking salts passing on the docks will remind you, if you bring up the subject, that the schooner *Bluenose* beat the Yankees every time! Indeed, in the International Cup Race

104

Unobtrusive Wedgeport: yet beyond in the open sea are the tuna grounds where yearly international championships are held and the fish caught weigh close to a thousand pounds.

Lighthouse at Pubnico Harbor. Besides, there is Upper Pubnico, Lower Pubnico, and Pubnico Center. Near Halifax there are several Musquodoboits; and there is more than one Brooklyn in Nova Scotia. Offshore is Cape Sable Island, "Graveyard of the Atlantic."

only once did the *Gertrude L. Thebaud,* the Massachusetts entry, take her measure, and that was in an exhibition series in 1930.

Fishermen races first flourished well back in the days when rival skippers tried to beat each other to port for the best prices for fresh fish. Contests between Gloucester and "Novy" fishermen began to attain prominence in the beginning of the century. In 1920 the Gloucester schooner *Esperanto,* with her great ability to sail "by the wind," beat the Canadian *Delawana* in two straight races. This was

Top left: Lobster buoys at Pubnico Harbor, extra long for visibility in the Nova Scotia altitudinous tides and waves. Top right: Yarmouth, full of its "Novey" type boats. Always plenty of glass in the cockpit and keels with holes for hauling up, and so they differ from the Jonesport boat. Bottom: In the Annapolis basin is Annapolis Royal, one of the oldest towns on this continent and the site of historic Fort Anne, which was captured and recaptured seven times. In 1854 the Duke of Kent rebuilt the old officer's quarters, today a museum filled with items of Acadian times. The immaculate parade grounds and ramparts are surmounted by old cannon; noteworthy is the nearby statue of handsome Sieur de Monts, leader of the settlement, 1604–13.

Alone in its glory, the Cathedral at St. Bernards in the French country on the coastal road toward Digby, where everyone seems to be named Comeau.

too much for the pride of the land of the Maple Leaf. A famous Haligonian marine designer was commissioned to draw plans for the *Bluenose,* which, of course, is the slang term for a virile Nova Scotian. His Excellency the Duke of Devonshire came down from Canada's capital city, Ottawa, for the keel-laying ceremonies and to drive the first spike. Pictures of the launching revealed the sweetness of her hull, and showed the crowds of Lunenburgers swarming around the ways.

The *Bluenose* turned out to be a freak of speed. Schooners built subsequently to her exact specifications have never been able to produce her amazing quality. Her architect, William Rose of Halifax, gazing in rapture as she cut the waves with beautiful ease would ask himself with abject humility, "I only wish I knew what makes her go."

The *Bluenose,* under her clever seasoned skipper, Angus Walters, defeated the

Left: The Digby shore. Beyond lies the Bear River country, side trip of beauty.
Right: At Lower Granville, a sidetrip of minutes from Annapolis Royal, is this life-
sized replica of the Habitation, small, dark, stockade-type buildings, tightly built
around a central court. This was the site of Champlain's Order of The Good Time
(1605), the first social club in North America, with membership certificates still
available to Nova Scotia visitors proving a few days sojourn. Here Lescarbot wrote
his *History of New France,* and produced on a floating barge the first play enacted
north of the Spanish Missions.

American schooners *Henry Ford* and the *Columbia* with considerable ease. During
the thirties, however, her races with the *Gertrude L. Thebaud* were for the most
part hard fought, often marked with acerbity and weird decisions. The *Thebaud,*
her first time out against the *Bluenose,* in the year of her launching, in an exhibition
series of two races, won both times by fifteen minutes and eight minutes respectively.
But that was the last defeat in a series for the *Bluenose.* She won all her International brushes with the Gloucester entry. In the last contest, held off Gloucester
in 1938, the *Thebaud* was defeated in a best three-out-of-five duel. The *Bluenose*
won the fifth and deciding race by two minutes, while the *Thebaud*'s racing skipper,
Ben Pine, stricken a few days before the final race, lay ashore in sick bay.

That year, after beating the Americans off Gloucester, Captain Angus Walter's
ire was aroused to a nonquotable pitch. The International Fisherman's Cup, which
had been displayed in the window of a Boston department store during the races,
was now lost en route to the victory banquet. Eventually the cup appeared. It
had been mysteriously left in the hall of the Home for Little Wanderers in the
city's South Huntington Avenue region. To add to the difficulties of sportsman-
ship, there was some trouble regarding the prize money reputedly belonging to the
Canadians.

The next year Angus Walters had another reason to be chagrined. An unpaid
bill for seven thousand dollars worth of marine engines made it seem certain that

108

This twice-a-day tidal embarrassment will be alleviated at the rate of a two-foot rise per hour.

the *Bluenose* would be sacrificed on the auction block. At the last moment Angus himself dug deep and came up with the required cash. "I still believe in the *Bluenose,*" was all he said.

Even the Bluenoses themselves tried to beat the *Bluenose*. A fast Nova Scotian boat, the *Haligonian,* designed by the same architect, raced her on occasion. Said a Lunenburger, speaking of the pretender, "She was a slippery piece of wood, to be sure. But she just couldn't beat the *Bluenose*. Nothing could."

Both the *Bluenose* and her arch rival sailed to a stirring welcome at the Chicago World's Fair in 1933, by way of the St. Lawrence and the Great Lakes. A few years later they were sold to separate firms doing a coasting business in the Caribbean. Both vessels were lost in more or less similar accidents. The *Bluenose,* as usual, went first. In 1946 the vessel that had once, years before, defied death off Sable Island and was saved by superior seamanship, now struck on a reef off Haiti. Her crew of eight were rescued. The *Thebaud* soon followed to her great reward when she came to grief in La Guayra, Venezuela, smashing on the breakwater of the harbor in a storm — to become a distinct menace to navigation. Lovers of both ships who knew their Conrad recalled his lines: "And this is all that is left of it. Only a moment; a moment of strength, of romance, of glamour — of youth! . . . A flick of sunshine upon a strange shore, the time to remember, the time for a sigh . . ."

It is impossible to forget the paneled dining room of that beautiful Lunenburg tavern decorated with porcelain and with the models of the *Bluenose* and in a glass case her great silver cup.

109

The French word Gaspé belongs to one of the largest towns on the peninsula almost fifty miles above Percé. There Cartier landed in 1534 and claimed the region for "Le Roy de France" and subsequently the entire peninsula has been called Gaspé by Americans and more correctly by French Canadians, "Gaspesia." "The tourist folders say it looks like Brittany," remarks our favorite lens and pen man, gay, witty, urbane Horace Sutton, author of the "Footloose" books. "But there are," he continues, "no women wearing tall white coifs, no men in cummerbunds and black velvet hats." Nonetheless, along this string of fishing villages you'll see dog carts, berets, and a plethora of churches, hear unbelievable French patois, envisage a wild beauty, sense a remoteness and quaintness impervious to the tick of time. By example is this photograph at Grande Rivière, a colorful Baie des Chaleurs town below Percé.

XI

South Shore Gaspé:
Baie des Chaleurs on Speedometer

TIME WAS when the best advice to the motorist about to circle the Gaspé was to start in the Rivière du Loup section of the St. Lawrence and keep to the inside, the clockwise way around. However, in recent years the improvement in the belt road — it is called the Perron Boulevard (and coming from Quebec you meet it at Ste. Flavie, well back on the St. Lawrence 85 miles east of Rivière du Loup) — has sent such warnings into the discard. Since this itinerary calls for a cease-driving at Quebec, we shall work down the peninsula east, up the Baie des Chaleurs and up the St. Lawrence River. The entire road is never unsafe, although it may be rough at times, especially above Percé.

From Matapédia to Percé, site of the famed Percé Rock (the pierced rock), will be a distance of about 180 miles; all the way to Quebec, approximately 670 miles. Of course, should we turn at right angles and follow the Matapédia Valley north to the St. Lawrence and Ste. Flavie, beginning (for us the end) of Gaspé's Perron, so-called "Boulevard"; the distance is only 90 miles. But in so doing we would saw off the peninsular Gaspesia, deprive ourselves of one of the most fascinating loop-the-loops in North America, because it is almost constantly in view of the sea and mountains. Yes, ahead is the poor man's trip to provincial France, with a touch of Norway and Switzerland thrown in, and no passport is needed.

Cartier's Baie des Chaleurs (bay of heats) was so named in 1534 when the explorer from St.-Malo, discouraged in his attempt to translate the mouth of the Restigouche River into an entrance to a Northwest Passage, came about and returned to the open sea, somewhat wilted in discouragement, deriving no refreshment from the unseasonable heat wave that gripped the Bay.

When our turn comes to take off eastward, up the shores of the Bay, which Cartier traveled by sea, the unfolding panorama will present gentle fields, receding woods, coves, and an occasional village. The road will be generally flat and easygoing as far as Percé. Most of the towns will be named for some former governor of Canada (military man or other important nabob) by a Micmac term, or for Saint Anne, the patron saint of the fishermen. Then there will be Anse-this and Anse-that, for "anse," after all, means cove. Children along the "Boulevard" — especially after the first hundred miles or so, when the country becomes less English and more French — will hold up for sale little wooden boats, berries, and other items of the *pays*. Gaspé urchins are in great profusion, and the bending clotheslines, tossing with white underwear shapes, like confetti in the breeze, indicate that the birth rate is astronomical. Not far from almost every back door is tethered the bulky work horse, who in no way resembles Native Dancer or other Kentucky Thoroughbreds, but is loved just as fondly. His aquatic counterpart in practicability, the fisher's sturdy boat, lies on its side in the marshes, awaiting sea duty.

At nearly all times on our right hand will be the Baie des Chaleurs. There will be fishermen at their gear or else ministering to their "flakes": low platforms of chicken wire, covered with split cod, drying under the summer sun. Cod is thus supposed to whiten best, and there are those who contend that this method makes the fish taste better too. Purse nets, gill nets, seines, old anchors, tackle, will edge the periphery of the coast. Before the black ribbon of a road winds up at Quebec City (at least two days of fast driving), we shall have passed through a score of covered bridges. These are especially frequent in the Chaleur region, carrying us across rivers about to meet the sea, streams undoubtedly harboring salmon. Fish

112

Moving across New Brunswick toward the Gaspé, and the junction of the Restigouche and Matapédia Rivers. A roadside shrine projects the realization that the French Canadian lives his constant belief, no matter how far from the urban manifestations of religion.

Left: Salmon river through a covered bridge, the Patapedia. Right: The Matapédia; tycoon and guides are discernible fishing valuable leased waters.

in storage, however, and, thanks to science, good for days to come, are represented in almost every village of size in this section by the *entrepôt frigorifique,* the local fish-freezing plant. As the curves add one upon the other, route warnings are in both French and English, such as "Ecole — School."

Near Percé the fields take on altitude. The promontories and the beaches show a vivid red cranberry color (very like the sands of the Parrsboro shore in upper Nova Scotia, the country around Cheticamp on Cape Breton, or the outer beaches of Prince Edward Island). The air will be perfumed by an aroma blend of white clover and the gently wafted air of drying cod. The inboard side of the road will offer a range of colors, if this be July and the wild flower season. Daisies will blanket the earth. Nor are they alone. A partial list of Gaspesian specimens would include: a God's-aplenty of clover, daisies, and dandelions, then aster, anemone, arbutus, bladder campion, cinquefoil, cowslip, cow vetch, cowbane, milkwort, ginseng, wild ginger, devil's-paintbrush, oxeye daisy, cow parsnip, false Solomon's-seal and Solomon's-seal, Queen Anne's lace, blue rushes, sea lungwort, red, pink, white, yellow water lilies, goldthread, eyebright, yellow dock, lamb's-quarters, spirea, jill-over-the-wall, and pyrola.

So much for a précis — obviously there is goodness ahead. But we must get back to our muttons to our starting line at the southwest corner of the Baie des Chaleurs.

Before shoving off at Matapédia, and prior to setting your speedometer at 00.0, we invite you to drive around town for a look-see at the salmon rivers. This is a corner of the world that one does not con every day, for all that it is well known to the millionaire who owns "salmon water." Here, where the Matapédia and Restigouche make a junction, is the site of the Restigouche Salmon Club, whose initiation fees are considered "reasonable enough"; members hold shares which are in the neighborhood of $5000 each, an extremely proper figure for the select twenty-five or so who belong. The usual picture is a guide and bowman for each, although not all members are in Canada at the same time, and a corps of caretakers police the five restricted areas owned by the club. The club makes certain that fishing sites are

South Shore Gaspé; Port Daniel, three attributes of Gaspesia: the faithful horse, the covered bridge (one of 24 on the tour), and the boatload of fishing gear.

rotated each year. Members draw for their positions and cackle over the results as if they were women at a bridge club.

Members of the Restigouche Salmon Club seldom have trouble in killing a fifteen- to twenty-pound salmon in season (the record, more than twice that poundage) between June 1 and August 15, in water that is auctioned every ten years. Millions of eggs are stripped off female salmon each year and carefully nurtured in hatcheries; babies are fed on liver, ground-up beef and lamb hearts, and then released. The Wall Street tycoon who dutifully ships a salmon in ice to his friends back in Westbury, Long Island, often pays about twenty dollars a pound for the privilege, figuring in all the overhead. However, as Bruce Hutchison has said, these are "probably the only happy and truly profitable days he is to know all year."

Along the peninsula there are streams emptying into the Bay that are open to the public. Somehow it seems the government has picked as "free" areas rivers

114

that never offer much in the way of fish. Nevertheless, it is possible to arrange some kind of fishing if your purse is fathoms deep. If that fine old hotel is still extant at Matapédia, all such mysteries may be explained. They treat the guest to every conceivable form of salmon on the menu, including breakfast. Here the tariff is low, the accommodation spotlessly clean.

So much for the local salmon rivers. Nor are they the last we shall see along the Gaspé. Since the forthcoming villages are hard to identify, because of an absence of township signs general on the Gaspé, for the ensuing pages we submit a motor guide — style Baedeker-like, terse and fragmentary. At least the accompanying schedule may assist you in determining your position on the highway, a road that was once an Indian portage.

(00.0) MATAPEDIA   We're off and running.

(6.5) RESTIGOUCHE   In Micmac the name originally signified a banzai-like battle cry meaning "disobey your father"; or it may stem from the Indian meaning, "river divided like a hand," with reference to the tributaries of the stream. Restigouche nonetheless was founded in 1820 as a Micmac mission, and became a pilgrimage honoring Saint Anne, a saint held in high esteem by the Micmacs, who in fact speak of her as their "queen." This quiet out-of-the-way spot was the site of a tempestuous naval rout. In 1760, before the days of modern communications, the king of France, not knowing that it was all over for France (Wolfe's victory at Quebec, 1759), had ordered a fleet to the capital as relief for the French defender, Lévis. This would-be armada met trouble in the form of British ships at the mouth of the St. Lawrence. The French fled south into the bottleneck at the end of the Baie des Chaleurs, the British at their heels. The pursuers were under the command of the poet Lord Byron's grandfather, John Byron, the so-called Foulweather Jack. The British victory, a long-drawn-out affair and a conquest of the already conquered, comes under the heading of a "posthumous battle."

(21.1) POINTE A LA GARDE   A short distance from Oak Bay on the main highway, Pointe à la Garde recalls the heroic defense of a fort here by Sieur Donat de la Garde, second officer of the French warship *Machault*. La Garde withstood a fierce bombardment by several British ships June 27–July 3, 1760, until forced to evacuate, the last naval battle in the Seven Years' War in North America.

(28.3) ESCUMINAC   Here are two great fish rivers, the Nouvelle and the Escuminac, both well stocked with large sea trout. Escuminac is from Indian meaning "lookout post" — an allusion to the heights dominating the village.

(35.5) ST. JEAN L'EVANGELISTE, also known as NOUVELLE   To the south the tip of Miguaska is visible — a part of Restigouche Bay. Battles by the dozen occurred in this area during the ancient French regime.

(41.0) ST. OMER   This attractive village dates from only 1899.

(47.0) TRACADIGECHE or CARLETON   The former name is Micmac for "home of the herons," and was changed to Carleton in honor of Governor-General Sir Guy Carleton (1786-96). Jacques Cartier is supposed to have erected a wooden cross here in 1534. A part of the population are descendants of the Acadians expelled by British from Nova Scotia in 1755. Loyalist refugees from the American Colonies during the War for Independence — Englishmen who chose to give up their worldly goods in the States rather than falter in allegiance to George III — also settled here.

(54.7) MARIA Named for Lady Dorchester, wife of a governor of Canada, this has been an Indian reservation almost one hundred years.

(62.3) NEW RICHMOND A thriving mining center is here, and one of the longest covered bridges on the continent. The covered bridge, which offered protection to its floorboards in snowstorms, represents a construction technique of wooden pins, bolts, and timbers, a know-how brought by the Loyalists from New England.

Cascapédia comes from an Indian word meaning "rapid streams." Both Little and Big Cascapédia Rivers are exempt of falls and rapids yet flow with great speed through their entire course. Both are famed for salmon, and may they long be protected from logging and pollution, menaces of salmon fishing. The Provincial government has now opened part of one river to all fishermen, until lately

116

Surrealism on the South Shore. Much is translated on roadside signs.

restricted to private angling. Salmon here are larger than in most rivers, the average being thirty pounds. Sixty-pounders have been killed; in 1887 the Marquis of Loine, former governor of Canada, and his party took as many as 320 salmon in the Cascapédias, one a forty-one-pounder.

The town was named for the Duke of Richmond, former governor-general of Canada, and is the gateway to the mineralized regions of the Shickshock Mountains toward Ste. Anne des Monts. The population is half English, half French, occupied by the usual farming, fishing, and lumbering.

(76.8) St. Charles de Caplan   "Where flax is superbly cultivated," says a local guide. This is chiefly an agricultural parish, founded in 1812. Caplan comes from "Capeland," from an Indian name, or possibly from a small fish found in the river, the *capelan* (capelin).

A Gaspesian guidebook insists that we give ear to the Legend of the Castaway Maiden: "As winds whistle in deep ravines and gorges between towering cliffs near the headland of Caplan, fishermen claim they hear moans and cries of 'Marguerite,' maiden of noble lineage, cast away on a rocky reef" long years ago. She was a passenger on ship to the newly discovered colony, a niece of the captain, who was a man of stern and rigorous principles. En route Marguerite fell in love with a young Norman, a man of the "common people." The uncle was outraged at his niece's conduct. She refused to heed him, and his fury passed all bounds. Steering his ship straight for land, he swung alongside a forlorn islet and there disembarked the fractious Marguerite and her lover, and set sail — never to rest his eyes on them again.

The young man eventually made a flimsy raft upon which he embarked, hoping the tide would carry him in shore. He never returned. Passing fishermen heard the girl's shrieks; they ferried mother and babe to the beach, but both died from their fearful experience.

Fishers still hear Marguerite's cries and indeed claim to have seen her spirit floating upon the crest of a wave in the pale moonlight.

(86.6) St. Bonaventure   Not to be confused with the island of Bonaventure near Percé, this village derives its name from the river at whose mouth it stands. Bonaventure River has its share of tributaries — the Hull, Duval, McGinnis, and Creux Rivers — and is well stocked with fish. The main river, in turn, took its name from the ship *Bonaventure* in which the Sieur de la Court Pré Ravillon sailed from France. This is another village settled by Acadians. These, however, were resolved to marry only among themselves. The records suggest that a certain Monsieur Foret left 318 descendants!

(97.2) New Carlisle   This village was established in 1783 and, like Douglastown, served as a refuge for Loyalists who fled the colonies during the Revolutionary War. It has been called "the only successful Loyalist settlement." At one time this was the terminal point of the peninsular railroad, which now extends to the town of Gaspé. The automobile road bends like a snake along this country and seems forever to be crossing and recrossing the railroad track. No train seems to appear however. In this industrial-commercial area the English-speaking populace support four churches of four separate faiths. The old Robitaille, full of historic souvenirs, is open to visitors.

101.6 Paspebiac   "Where cod makes his appearance," says an old guidebook. Here is the headquarters of those famous general stores that all look alike and are to be seen everywhere on the Gaspé — the chain of Robin, Jones and Whitman. Robin, the founder of the firm, started his business life as a fisherman from Paspébiac about the time of the American Revolution. In 1776 American privateers raised havoc with his boats, although the British Navy later recaptured some of them. Robin made a strong financial comeback after the war, having merged his enterprises with Jones and Whitman. Their twentieth-century selling interests include such items as postcards and souvenir pottery.

Paspébiac in Micmac means "divided shallows," or "broken shoal" — a reference to the natural formation at the entrance of the harbor. This is one of the oldest parishes in the district, dating back to 1796. It is an important fishing port and also an industrial area.

(119.5) PORT DANIEL   It is true enough that Jacques Cartier found the heat of July taxing when he sailed into the Baie des Chaleurs in 1534, but were he to return to a village like Port Daniel today, he might wonder why so many houses have second-story doors. Sometimes the snowstorms pile up to a twenty-five-foot height. It is then the little door is used for egress.

This town bears the name of a French sailor of Champlain's day. A picturesque port, with its prominent *entrepôt frigorifique*.

(125.0) ANSE AUX GASCONS   Here is the actual entrance to the Baie des Chaleurs. Pebbles found here are called "Gaspé stones" — they are jasper or cornelian.

The town legend records that in early days a ship was wrecked off Percé and a member of the crew, who was from Gascony, lashed himself to a piece of the wreckage. He was carried far down the coast to this bay, where he crawled to safety on the beach. He was aided by fishermen who found him on the sands; the event supplied the name. CAP D'ESPOIR   This cape owes its name to Jacques Cartier. A Gaspé guidebook advances the legend of the phantom ship, a local "Flying Dutchman," which visits this part of the coast at least once a year. It is generally seen in summer twilight, on a calm sea, when huge waves suddenly rise from the bottom of the ocean and tumble toward the beach. Out of these agitated foam-covered combers there looms the ghostly form of a vessel, all sails set, steering for the breakers at the foot of the Cape. The deck is said to be manned by sailors and soldiers dressed in the garb of olden times. "On the prow stands the captain, a white draped form on his left arm. . . . Wind howls, sea rages, a clap of thunder, crashing noise, and the vessel and her ghostly crew are no more! A few piercing cries, among which can be heard that of a woman — then silence and calm."

(132.0) NEWPORT   "Where fishing is most abundant" — and the railroad activity seems important.

(143) CHANDLER   Huge paper mill metropolis named for a Philadelphian. Commerciality rears its head, quaintness is blotted out, but undoubtedly the townsfolk make a better wage than their fisher neighbors.

(147) PABOS   "One of the oldest stations of the coast."

(152) GRANDE-RIVIERE   Where the motorist should descend from his car and photograph the native fishing activity.

(162.7) ANSE A BEAUFILS   The "stepson's cove" is so called because a young black sheep of an ancient French family, exiled from his country, lived here in the early days and attracted considerable attention owing to uncertainty of his birth. He was suspected of having been a stepson of a man "quite close to the reigning King of France." This is an important fishing village and extremely picturesque mecca for artists.

(169.1) PERCE   The peak of the Gaspé tour is worthy of a chapter by itself.

Nearing Percé, a man-created "Barachois-like" harbor. These fishing boats resemble our old double-ended pinkies. A smart handling vessel, but difficult in a following sea.

There she is! The Rock of Percé seen from the Anse du Sud.

XII

Percé, Peak of the Gaspé Tour

PERCE, SINCE IT IS LOCATED just at the underside of the mouth of the St. Lawrence, can in its position be compared to historic Castine, Maine, which was at the other end of Acadia. In those days of uninterrupted war, almost everything happened to Castine because it was on a direct line between Nova Scotia and Boston, as well as being a sheltered harbor hung at the entrance of a great river. Percé has seen more grief than the Canal Turn of the Grand National Steeplechase. Horses haven't tumbled here, but missions, crosses, churches, and fisheries have. With the English, Dutch, and renegade French furrowing the seas — rovers whose sole purpose was to plunder the vessels and the posts of the enemy — Percé was on the corner of a busy street.

Perhaps you recall the zany expression that used to appear in chalk on every post and fence a few years back: "Kilroy was here." Kilroy would have had a hard time pre-empting Jacques Cartier of St.-Malo, Brittany, who was first in his pet territory, from Prince Edward Island, the Baie des Chaleurs, and Quebec. These waters were his oyster and he proved it by writing it down when he arrived home. Cartier makes sure that we consider him first at Percé — or Percy as the English call it. "Being certain," writes Cartier, "that there was no passage through this bay [Chaleur Bay] we made sail and set forth [from Port Daniel on Sunday, July 12] in order to explore and discover beyond this bay as far as Cape Pratto . . ." Some feel that the original appellation comes from the Right Reverend Albert de Pratto, Canon of London, who accompanied John Rut in 1527 on his expedition to New Foundland, when they presumably visited these coasts. In any case Canon Pratto reported back to Cardinal Wolsey in London. To this day one of the lesser promontories at Percé is called Cape Canon.

Cartier's follow-up-man, Samuel de Champlain, was of more recent date, and his records are more articulate and available. He arrived at Percé, just as he did at Quebec about seventy years after Cartier. Champlain got the credit for founding, although not discovering, Quebec; at Percé he is acknowledged only for naming the spot. In 1603, the year before he visited Port Royal (Annapolis Royal) and Mount Desert Island, he wrote: "We came to Percé Island which is really a high rock . . . where there is a hole" — the "pierced rock."

Since Cartier's coming the rock had been completely severed from the mainland and undoubtedly the famous arch within the rock had been formed. With Champlain, the term Isle Percé is evolved: the rock was surrounded by water at high

One can walk dry-shod below the great rock at low tide and gaze up at millions of pounds of conglomerate. The white specks are not scratches in the negative, but wheeling gulls and other birds. Left: Guide Duval en route to Bonaventure, his ancestral island. Right: A close-up view of hole in the great rock of Percé.

tide. After 1850 the cumbersome "Isle" was dropped; the word Percé alone has prevailed.

For the traveler at Percé today there is much to evaluate. Since accommodations are clean and comfortable and available at all prices, this is the place to rest both tires and brakes, body and soul. Glowing as will be the dénouement to Quebec City — here is the culmination of the entire trip. Percé is the jewel of the ring; the Baie des Chaleurs the facet on the lower, the south side; the St. Lawrence River the upper part of the band. South shore and north shore divide at Percé, each, in its own way, so lovely and so different.

Percé has triple-feature appeal: the Rock, Mont Ste. Anne, and Bonaventure Island. Secondary are Pic d'Aurore, Mont Joli, the Three Sisters, Anse du Sud, Anse du Nord, the Hill of Surprise. Back in the hills, Percé, home of the cod, nonetheless can offer fresh-water fishing.

Consider Quebec and its citadel — one visualizes a giant rock bulking straight up and topped by a hotel. Recall Gibraltar, and there is a mental picture of a fortified rock, made famous by the advertising of an American insurance company. But envision Percé and there is the connotation of a rock on a remote coast existing for the sake of its beauty alone, its only tenants a smoke of birds soaring and wheeling above its flush deck.

Not only does Percé Rock have distinguished shape but it has texture and hue. The sun uses its reflector surface like a vast palate, or an outdoor movie screen, and sends the color-range climbing, with every mood of the day. And as for its form, either in the mists of early morn or by moonlight, there is always the monumental silhouette.

For the photographer of ships who prefers the aircraft carrier hull to any other, Percé offers the same appeal. It takes little effort to imagine the Rock a wounded carrier, bow to shore, beached on an even keel — withal it has lost its control-island topside, and part of its stern, codicil-like, trails abaft. And it is as if the shape has taken a giant torpedo beyond the poop, a "fish" that passed gaily through the compartmented ship and seaward, leaving a vast hole 60 feet high and 100 feet wide. The planes are no longer stacked on the flight deck, their place taken by myriad wings of a smaller nature — Percé birds soaring and calling, seldom coming in for a landing.

The rock is 1420 feet long and including the obelisk, 1555 feet. It is 300 feet wide at its widest point, which is the western, mainland end, and 288 feet high, receding somewhat in height as it streamlines back to its stern. The weight above the waterline, an estimated four million tons, is considerably more than the heaviest aircraft carrier, whose over-all displacement would not exceed forty thousand tons. From the inexorable erosion of the waves and frost the rock is disintegrating at a rate of 300 tons yearly. Yet scientists conservatively estimate that there will be something to see for 13,000 years. In Cartier's day the distance between the point of the rock and the high bank called Mont Joli was not surrounded by water, even at high tide; what Cartier saw consequently was a peninsula. But in the years before the arrival of Champlain, the water had broken through and it became the Isle Percé. Today, one may reach the rock dry-shod at low tide unless they may be frightened by the possibility of a sudden mass erosion. Fear-gripped Béchard, when he looked straight up at the rock in 1857. "I felt ill at ease," he wrote, "as going about this lofty rock on foot and perceive

123

suspended above your head this enormous mass which seemingly wants to crush you."

Geologists have long been enraptured by the properties of the rock. John M. Clarke, one of the more famous in that field, coined the name Percésia to describe this section around Percé. In his ecstasy — almost unbecoming for a scientist — he puts aside terminology like "Paleozoic beds," "glacial clay," "sandstones of the Quarternary era," and becomes persuasively lyric regarding the colors of the rock. "Its walls are bathed in tints of purple, red, bright yellow, and gray-blue" (this is Clarke speaking) ". . . the natural shades of the limestone, and these are diversified by great strokes of white calcite that vein the mass. On its top the green carpet of grass spreads downward as the slopes permit, while over the jagged anfractuosities near the summit a deep orange-red lichen has added its color to the scheme." Obviously the honorable geologist was sold on the rock. But he is not alone. Pye, in the eighteen hundreds, called it "one of the most remarkable objects on the entire Canadian coast. One of the most extraordinary monuments of the Almighty Architect." Artists have ever given the famous shape the full treatment: in oils, pastels, watercolor, pencil, pen. The sellers of artists' material have good reason to bless the rock.

The white birds at the top of the rock object to all winged outsiders from the greater population of the bird sanctuary on yonder Bonaventure Island. Undoubtedly they would resent man too — if he were able to climb the heights. Today a law prevents the impossible. In the old days, however, it is reported that three tons of hay were harvested from the top of the rock yearly.

One of the early legends pertains to a sailor madly in love with a Percé brunette. Just prior to his ship's clearing port, the determined lover, who must have had strong fingernails, somehow ascended the rock, and undoubtedly lay flat in a crevice. Gun volleys from the search parties sent by the captain of his vessel failed to dislodge him. After his ship had disappeared well under the horizon, he descended, joined the brunette on shore, and gleefully celebrated his nuptials.

One of the most important artists' renditions was produced by a Captain Hervey Smythe. At the time Smythe, as Wolfe's aide-de-camp, was on his way in 1758 to assail the heights of Quebec. (This military man must have been versatile, for his

124

Left: Percé, distinctive office of the Canadian National Bank. Right: Removing all night protection for a fine day's drying in the sun.

Gannets on Bonaventure. The island off of Percé is one of the great, if not the greatest, bird sanctuaries of the entire world.

Percé sketch is only one of several artistic contributions that he made while in Canada.) In his "Rock of Percé," which shows Wolfe's frigate in the foreground, the composition presents clear evidence that the rock formerly had two arches. Parliament liked Smythe's drawing so well that authorization was given to print it from copperplate.

On the seventh of June 1847, inhabitants of the village of Percé heard a devastating burst of sound and saw an atomic cloud of dust topped with swarms of clamorous birds. One of the arches of the rock had fallen, leaving but one hole. This is as we see it today.

At Percé on the occasion of the Feast of Saint Peter, patron saint of the fishermen, the blessing of the boats takes place about the time of the pilgrimage to Mont Ste. Anne. The procession heads toward the sea, to the reciting of prayers and the chanting of hymns. A silver cross spearheads the little band, followed by the curate in purple surrounded by altar boys. On arrival at the water's edge the curate is taken aboard on one of the fishing craft. Standing in the prow, prayerbook in hand, he is ferried from boat to boat, each craft decked out in flowers and flags, each hull perhaps of a different hue. The words are said over each boat and the sign is made. Those gathered on shore for the ceremony are led in prayer by a priest. Eventually the procession enters the church. Curé Roy, in his guide-

Recording of the morning sun at Percé just as it touches land on its long day's
journey westward across a continent.

book of Percé, closes his description of the ceremony with: "Each one returns
with the conviction that tomorrow the catch will be better, the effort less costly,
the daily burden less onerous, because on his boat the blessing of the Lord has
descended."

Fourteen hundred feet in altitude, Mont Ste. Anne is accessible only from the
north side. The other three sides are sheer cliffs. Many a fisherman, as far away
as 75 miles, owes his life to the mountain, for he has been able to determine his
position when the summit of Ste. Anne has appeared in his range of vision. From
the mountaintop itself the panorama is unadulterated picture-postcard stuff — even

Anticosti Island shows up from its great distance. Below, the birds wheeling over the Rock, the village of Percé and the island of Bonaventure are scarcely perceptible, but the shapes of the monuments themselves stand out in sharp relief.

From the beginning, Mont Ste. Anne has been a center for pious gatherings. Wood and material have been hauled by oxen and carried on men's backs for the erection of shrines and crosses on its remote summit. Too often they have fallen in ruins during gales of wind. But in 1935 a seemingly permanent monument was erected by fervent devotees of Saint Anne.

To the rear and even higher is La Montagne Blanche with its Grande Crevasse, where wild saxifrage grows, a hundred-foot-deep fissure — seven feet wide at its opening, narrowing like a wedge at the bottom. Also there is the smaller, La Petite Crevasse. Add to this a wild grotto, a brook of waterfalls, and caves full of stalactites and stalagmites. Throughout this wonder paradise of the botanist, trails have been carefully laid out and maintained by lovers of this sacred mountain.

Bonaventure Island gives the impression of a giant whale stranded on a reef — in fact the name "Black Whale" appears on the front of a shop in Percé. Clarke called it an "oval green rug." This island, three miles offshore, six miles in circumference, was named Bonaventure by Cartier in honor of the "Seraphic Doctor," Saint Bonaventure, whose feast day (July 4) he anticipated as he lay at anchor in the second week of July 1534.

The waves of the open sea smash against the cliffs of Bonaventure and except for two small coves on the west side, landing on the island is difficult — in fact impossible in stormy weather. It is more suited for the raising of sheep than for crops, but there is never a shortage of wild flowers in season. For those seeking the bird sanctuaries on the outer side, the ample woodland makes it difficult to follow a straight trail across the island. The ground cover is utterly charming, however, and Nicolas Denys in his *Histoire Naturelle* said: ". . . rabbit hunting was good, thirty snares set the night before yielding at least twenty rabbits the next morning; turtle doves abound here because of the great quantity of strawberries and raspberries of which they are very fond." The fathoms of sea that slap against the rock sides of the island have gouged out Capri-like grottoes, caves that once supposedly offered safe keeping for the booty hidden by corsairs and pirates. Even without its section of screaming feathered life, the island would by itself have copious charms. Its population has never been more than 200 people.

The Bonaventure bird sanctuary has given the island international importance. Living on dizzy cliffs an area of a half-mile long, a hundred feet high in almost perfect harmony, despite the varied species, are perhaps a hundred thousand auks, kittiwakes, puffins, herring gulls, penguins, petrels, cormorants, gannets and razor-billed auks. The gannets cry *currach, currach*. The double-crested cormorant merely grunts. The herring gull goes *kek-kek*. The kittiwake's sound is just like its name.

The birds follow the arrival of the herring in the spring. Eggs are laid in May and are hatched a month later. The young birds, if they are gulls, take off on their own in July; the cormorant, who swims under water with such ease, sails off in August; the baby gannets and razor-billed auks test their wings in September. Once their little wings are wet they rise with difficulty from the sea and generally have to wait for the sun to dry them before they can fly again. The elder gannets and the cormorants digest the food for their youngsters, then store it in an inside sack like the external pouch of the pelican.

The mature gull has an adroit way of using the force of gravity to crack the hard shell of crustaceans. Holding the unfortunate bivalve in his claws he sadistically flies up with his victim and then drops it to the rocks below as many times as is necessary to crack well before eating.

The great black-backed gull is the only outlaw in the spectacle of the cliffs. Rapacious and lazy, he sometimes throws his five-pound weight around. Unlike the others, he does not dive for his supper, but often devours everything in his reach, even the young of other families. Fortunately for the less aggressive kind, his tribe doth not increase; the gannets and the herring gulls outnumber him twenty to one, the cormorant five to one. The kittiwake doesn't dive much either, but subsists on the plant and animal life — the plankton — which floats upon the surface. So much fish is devoured by the birds from the Bonaventure cliffs one would think that the poor pisces would move away. Despite the fact that the gannet eats his own weight in fish daily, there seems to be God's plenty for both bird and man.

Whereas Percé has always greeted happily its sufficiency of visitors, there have been times in history when the tourists were just too much for the year-round residents. Apparently Phips's able-bodied soldiers did not fit any of the classifications mentioned by the Father. En route to Quebec some of the Phips frigates descended on the mission at Percé with a display of acute vandalism, "the re-

128

Gaspesian loom — one-woman operation.

sponsibilities for which no one wishes to accept." In a most pathetic letter written to his superior, articulate Father Jumeau, the last Recollet missionary to Percé, reveals some of the atrocities of 1690. (This was the year that Phips and his thirty-five vessels were obliged to retreat from Quebec in complete disorder when Governor Frontenac decided to reply "by the mouth of his cannon.")

My Reverend Father — I pass over in silence the harrowing details of the shipwreck which we experienced last year, in a terrible night on the twenty-third day of November, against the Cap des Rosiers, fifteen leagues from Isle Percé, and of the misfortune which we have suffered this year, in our capture by a privateer of Flessingue at fifty leagues from La Rochelle. . . . It seems as if our Lord had willed to have my life on the shipwreck only in order that I might be the witness of the total ruin and entire desolation of this place so that I could myself give you an account thereof. . . . I need only tell you that at the commencement of the month of August last, two English frigates appeared in the roadstead of the Isle of Bonaventure flying the standard of France, and through this stratagem, they easily seized five fishing vessels whose captains and crews . . . remained for eight entire days, during which they committed a hundred impieties. . . . And among other things they robbed, ravaged, and burnt the houses of the residents, who number at least *eight to ten families,* and who, for the most part had already taken refuge hurriedly in the woods. . . . I shudder with horror at the simple recollection of the impieties and sacrileges committed by these villains in our church, which they used as a guardhouse and as a place of debauchery . . . they shattered our images, trampled them under foot. . . . The pictures of the Holy Virgin and of Saint Peter were not exempt from their fury, nor from their passions, for both of these were riddled with more than a hundred and fifty gun shots. . . . The sacrileges of Baltazar who, in olden times in the midst of a festival, profaned the sacred vessels of the Temple of Jerusalem by making his courtesans and his concubines drink therefrom, were the same as those committed by these heretics, who, in the midst of their horrible debaucheries, extending through day and night, drank from our chalices their bumpers to the health of the Prince of Orange. . . . They took the crowns of the Holy Sacrament, and of the Blessed Virgin, and placed them upon the head of a sheep; they tied the feet of this animal, and having laid it down upon the consecrated stone of the high altar, they slaughtered it, and offered it in sacrifice, in derision of the sacrifice of the Holy Mass. . . . They then set fire to the four corners of the church, which was soon reduced to ashes, as was likewise the church of our Mission in the Isle Bonaventure, which had also a similar fate after they had shattered the image and slashed all the ornaments with heavy sabre cuts.

An attempt has been made to affix the blame for this unfortunate raid on a certain William Mason. We are told that Boston has been anxious to prove that Mason's venture was prompted by New York interests. Historians seem to feel in all fairness to Phips that the order did not come from either him or his immediate subordinates.

Piracy was again to appear on the shores of Percé during the Revolution and the War of 1812. Again the acts were committed by the "Bostonians." And Charles Robin and his brother John write of the boats seized in 1777 which included barrels of codfish and stocks of goods lost to American pirates.

The last leg. Cartier saw all this and Quebec too around 1500. Leaving Percé we must first ascend Mont Ste. Anne (left in picture), wave farewell to the Three Sisters (center), and Mont Joli (right). Photograph taken from Anse du Nord (foreground).

XIII

North Shore Gaspé — Up Along the St. Lawrence — More Miles and Tenths

ON THE GO again — and "up along" (as they say in Canada) the north shore of the Gaspé "Peninsular." As for the views ahead: in the words of an American ale advertisement: "Expect something wonderfully different."

The population and the thinking and speaking will now be French, predominantly and provincially. Occasionally on festive fishing boats is seen the tricolor of France or more often by a dooryard the light blue flag of Quebec province with its fleur-de-lis; not for some time will British bunting reappear. The swing west will have a European flavor, what MacKinley Helm calls the "channel manner."

The countryside will be higher and more rough hewn. Spurs and low hills of ribbed black shale will, at times, border the road. Promontories close by our elbow will replace the easygoing fields of the Baie des Chaleurs; topside, perhaps, a forest-decked hillside on the edge of a mountain pitch, a lumberman's hut or the patchwork quilt pattern of tiny farms, fenced and walled off as are the areas on the mountains of Yugoslavia on the Dalmatian coast. Over the decades, fathers have parceled out these awkward sections of ground to their sons, who in turn have made the best of their meager inheritance.

As we pull up and out of Percé, straightway flush in the face of the radiator cap the road will ascend 1300 feet in a mile and a half. As far as the road itself is concerned, however, climbs for the balance of the tour will not be precipitous, but altitudes for a couple of hundred miles will be respectable. The old taboo, however, regarding the counterclockwise, west-east circumvention of the Gaspé has, with the improvement of the highway, passed into the discard. Much of the time the road does not attempt to scale the heights, but weaves through or below the coastal saddles, along the beaches and coves. The mighty Shickshocks provide, it is true, the postcard setting, but driving close by their vicinity is as safe as in Central Park, except that there are no traffic lights or policemen.

Books of import have been written about the geology of this area. The essential fact for the layman is that the Shickshock Mountains (Micmac Indian for high, sharp points) are an extended part of the Appalachian Range that curves up from Vermont to taper off into a thin finger of limestone at Cape Gaspé, a finger that is only a half mile wide where it emerges from the mainland. Mont Jacques Cartier, the highest peak in the Shickshocks, nearly 5000 feet high, taller than any summit in the Laurentians, appears in view from Ste. Anne des Monts.

Our route has no direct traffic with this distant Shangri-La, however. The grades we pass over so happily with proper banking and protection seem not as high as they measure. At Grand Ruisseau, between Grande Vallée and Madeleine, it is only 800 feet, at Marsouins, 2000 feet, at Ruisseau Vallée, 2600, and at Petit Cap, 500. If the fog is not barring our view, the vistas are magnificent. Loveliest perhaps of any of the mountainous curving bays are those snuggling villages of Mont St. Pierre and Mont St. Louis, the latter named not for Saint Louis but for its river flowing between the mountains, so called in honor of Louis XIV.

Mont St. Louis, one of the oldest villages on the North Shore, is at 1800 feet and lies at the foot of its dark high mountains. When General Wolfe's men sacked it on their way to Quebec, it was even then one of the most important fishing hamlets on the peninsula.

Adjacent Mont St. Pierre is 1600 feet high and some feel that no words describe its somber beauty, lying at the end of a crescent bay between two curvaceous summits, a composition resembling in a rougher way much of what is felt from the encircling road dropping down from Hyères into Cannes on the French Riviera. This is Gaspesian composition, a cruder stage set, whose background mountains are covered with forests except for patches here and there swept by landslides — at the bottom, the inevitable little cluster of fishermen's houses.

Having established the contrast with the south shore in the matter of altitude, many features nonetheless will be the same. High road or low, there will be the same wild flowers, especially if the visitor arrives in the month of July: the senses will again be picked up by an aroma of red or white clover, and a dash of cod, a solid he-perfume and as pungent and bracing as a slight whiff of oxygen. The sight will be pleased by scatterings of purple and blue vetch, daisies, butter-and-egg, and yellow devil's-paintbrush. The gray road will skirt close by fishers at their flaking tables or tubs, cleaning the cod, dispatching the valuable livers, employing the same methods of Nicolas Denys, fisherman seigneur, on the same beaches some three hundred years ago. Descendants of medieval gulls tumble in pinwheel turns, screeching and crying voraciously as they snatch, almost from the hand of le pêcheur, the offal and discarded parts of fish.

And in nearly every village the large Catholic church with its steeple almost invariably covered with aluminum paint. Children everywhere, bursting out all over the landscape in or nearby the villages, rivaling only the wild flowers in their numbers; a barbed wit has said that Gaspesian winters are so long, so cold, that the urchins are not "cut out of their underwear" until July — undoubtedly there's proof in such statements by the numbers of small white under garments on sagging clotheslines, whipped by the warm river breeze.

Often surrounding the houses are walls of firewood, fodder for below zero winters to come; our seven-league-boots pace doesn't permit peering within the modest dwellings to see the huge nickel-plated stove, procured by the mail order catalogue; like the Nuremberg Stove, heart and hearthside of the house in Gaspesia almost five sixths of the year.

Fast as we may be traveling, the genial *enfants,* whose smiles could benefit by use of Pepsodent, cause us to pull to a stop. But conversation, whether your French was practiced on a Paris taxi driver or embellished at the Sorbonne, gets you not very far. Their patois is a tongue beyond all deciphering — English will often work better. After all, so many children say *char* for automobile, *gaz* for the French *essence* (gasoline). Don't strain, linguistically.

132

Over many generations the Gaspesians themselves have fallen prey to a corruption of their own names and sounds. Sieur de Monts du Gast lost some immortality in two instances — in the memory of Ste. Anne des Monts and Cap Chat. His grateful protégé, Champlain, when up in these parts, called, for his Huguenot patron, one spot "Pointe de Monts" (despite the mountains beyond, there wasn't even a nubbin along the beach point). But understandably Champlain's effort went, in time, into discard; the de became des and the Monts could mean the Monts behind the town; with the patron saint of the fishermen mixed in, out came Ste. Anne des Monts.

As for Cap du Gast, some of its rocks looked so much like a feline to a wealthy and influential citizen of a later day that the place became Cap Chat; today it's a lumber town.

Fortunately for posterity, the Sieur de Monts' handsome features, goateed and mustachioed, are sculptured, with plenty of accompanying credit for his exploits, atop a shaft at Annapolis Royal; and his name has been given to a manicured spring in Acadia National Park in Bar Harbor, Maine.

All of which reminds us that, whether the road ahead dips low or high, there are other explorers who got to Quebec afore us — Cartier, Champlain, Phips, Kirke, and the rest. From the high prows of their vessels in the adjacent St. Lawrence while doing five knots they never saw one tithe of what the motorist will see, no matter how much the windshield is plastered with squashed bugs and

Gaspesian waterworks, North Shore.

133

dust, and at a considerably greater number of land miles per hour.

(176.7) COIN DU BANC This is a charming village, we're told.

(182.9) BARACHOIS Its name denotes an especial characteristic of Gaspé's bays — the sandbar (Indian corruption of *barre,* bar, and *échouer,* to run aground). Here the heights present a panorama of incomparable grandeur, and Bonaventure Island shows up in its black whale shape. Eighteen moose were once shot in this vicinity, and local salmon have been known to be of monstrous size.

(191.1) ST. GEORGES DE LA MALABAIE Fishing and farming are pre-eminent here.

(198.1) FORT PREVEL This small Provincial park bearing the name of a Gaspé soldier who fell on the field of battle during the last war occupies the site of a former military camp.

(202.7) DOUGLASTOWN Named in honor of a British rear admiral, it was founded by an Englishman whose flock included Colonists remaining loyal to the English crown during the American Revolution and forsaking their homes in New York, Massachusetts, and elsewhere to seek opportunity on the Gaspé. Hopes were high as they planned their city; old maps of town planners revealed land set aside for parks, schools, churches, and administration buildings, but their plans never materialized. Fifty years later a wave of Irish-immigrants poured into Douglastown.

(219.0) GASPE According to the best authorities the name derives from the word Gaspeg, meaning "land's end." Over four hundred years ago, in the presence

134

Near Fox River, Gaspé coast.

of Indians who gathered to watch the arrival of white man, Cartier erected a large wooden cross and took possession of the land in the name of his king. *Vive le Roi de France!*

Gaspé, five hundred miles closer to Europe than Montreal, might have been one of the famous havens in the world. Apparently the harbor neither needs dredging nor has much embarrassment from fog. In 1628 Admiral Kirke and the British Fleet overtook Roquemont, the French commander, in Gaspé Bay, burning his vessels, which were loaded with supplies for Quebec, and at the same time capturing enormous booty. Wolfe, who spent some time here en route to Quebec, is remembered for the heavy-handed actions of his men and for the old house he occupied, now in ruins. Today Gaspé, a bishopric, is mostly English-speaking and is important for its commercial atmosphere (lumbering and sawmills) and its hospital. Gaspé was a Canadian embarkation point for transports in World War II.

(224.8) ST. MAJORIQUE Founded in 1876, this is an agricultural community.

(232.2) PENOUILLE This was a trading post during the French regime.

(237.2) CAPE AUX OS The name means cape of bones — so called because whalebones were found on the rocky shore. Occupies a site where Cartier's ships anchored for a peaceful visit, to be followed over two centuries later by a military conquest by Wolfe. CAP BON AMI This is a magnificent lookout spot. POINTE DU FORILLON, whose tip is the Cape of Gaspé, may be seen from here.

(244.1) CAP DES ROSIERS This area of land, of which Cap des Rosiers is one of the most extreme points, was known to earliest explorers as the Forillon — a word derived from the verb *forer* (to pierce, bore, drill). The fact that it bores its way into the ocean justifies this name. On some English maps Forillon appears as "The Flower Pot." The name Cap des Rosiers appears on a Champlain map of 1632, alluding to a great cliff covered with wild rosebushes.

(255.9) ANSE A LA FOUGERE A small fishing village is found here. ANSE AU GRIFFON This is noted, of course, for its church. *Griffon* was the name of a vessel commanded by a descendant of Nicolas Denys, the first seignior who commanded all the rights from Canso to this point. The name may possibly evolve from "Anse au Gris Fond" (gray-bottom cove), because the lucid water shows so clearly the gray sand beneath. ANSE JERSEY was settled originally by fishermen from the Jersey Islands.

(256.5) RIVIERE AUX RENARDS Foxes were numerous on the banks when English-speaking settlers called it Fox River. Because of the wreck of an Irish immigrant ship in 1847, many of the descendants of the castaways bear Irish names. They no longer speak the Celtic tongue. The name appears on maps as early as 1744.

This was the scene of the first fishermen's strike on the Gaspé. It was 1909 and conditions were poor in the area; one of the locals returned from the states with stories of how labor there achieved its ends. As the walkout continued, the unorganized fishers plundered company stores and property. Troops landed from government cruisers quickly ended the uprising.

Fox River had its troubles, too, in World War II. Its cod had been usually sold to Italy, but when Britain brought sanctions against Mussolini, the Italians refused to conduct business with English firms. Though thousands of miles from Number 10 Downing Street, this small village felt the effect of international politics.

(263.3) L'ECHOURIE This town is so called because at low tide fishing boats are stranded on their sides (*échoués*) for long periods. Good shooting and fishing in and near village limits. A beautiful lake (Lac de l'Echouerie) is about a quarter-mile from town and can be reached over a good road. Grand Lac de l'Echouerie, a mile and a half from the church, also offers splendid fishing. The government maintains a powerful Marconi and signal station here.

Considerable squid fishing. Fishermen use squid for bait when in search of cod and, according to those who should know, the squid unfortunately is also one of the favorite foods of the porpoise.

(283.2) St. Yvon   A German torpedo exploded here in 1942. As can be seen, it did no damage. Grand Etang is on an attractive lake surrounded by hills, and L'Anse a Valleau is a typical fishing village.

(287.0) Cloridorme   The name is a mispronunciation of the Christian name of a former resident, Coridon Cote. A World War II ship was sunk here by a German submarine. Cloridorme's church is especially imposing.

(291.5) Pointe a la Fregate   This point is so called because a warship pounded to pieces two hundred years ago. Parts of its ancient cannon can be seen at nearby Anse aux Canons.

(301.2) Grande Vallee   Here is a soothing view for the weary motorist, and a superb sand beach. Also ideal for short boat trips because it is well sheltered from the winds by great cliffs and promontories. Petite Vallee   We take time out for another myth, the Legend of Rose La Tulippe, told by a local fisherman.

(314.4) Petite Madeleine and Madeleine   These towns are fishing ports. Madeleine formed part of the seigniory acquired in 1723 by the celebrated botanist, Michel Sarrasin.

(317.6) Manche d'Epee   The finding of an ancient French rapier hilt buried here gave the place its name. It is the highest point on the Boulevard, yet has a sufficiently wide road.

(325.4) Gros Morne   A church built on top a massive cape — the name means "great knoll" — marks this.

(328.5) Anse Pleureuse   This small village has a big legend. Breton settlers who landed here in the early eighteen hundreds heard ghostly sounds from the nearby woods, a moaning or weeping — a *pleureuse* — late each night. One day an *abbé* by the name of Painchaud (hot bread) ventured through the village. Delayed because of a storm, he soon learned of the spine-chilling moans that came from the woods. A man of action was the good *abbé,* for he took a hatchet and plunged into the woods. Deep in the forest he came upon the ghostly source of the moans, merely a clump of trees that brushed against each other when the wind blew and created what the villagers had believed were cries of woe. When the *abbé* emerged from the village, he deemed it sufficient to say only that they would no longer be bothered by the ghost of the forest.

(332.5) Mont Louis   Breathtaking in its beauty, Mont Louis once formed part of an ancient seigniory, named in honor of Louis XIV. To the southwest rises the highest summit of the Shickshock chain — Mont Jacques Cartier, 4170 feet high. Local fish have been shipped all over the world, especially to Genoa, Marseilles, and Barcelona.

(344.1) Ruisseau Arbour   This is an attractive village, and Riviere a Claude has its charming church. Mont St. Pierre is set in a bay of beautiful beaches at the foot of high tree-crested cliffs. Water a lovely emerald color, reflected from the green summits. Could be Switzerland.

(349.9) MARSOUINS   The name is taken from Micmac meaning "stone for fire" or French *marsouin* (porpoise), the latter representing a threat to cod fishing all along the coast.

(362.7) RUISSEAU CASTOR, CAP AUX RENARDS, RIVIERE A LA MARTRE   These are picturesque farming and fishing villages.

(365.9) ST. JOACHIM DE TOURELLE   *Tourelle* derives from the form of a local turret-like rock here, which will be eroded completely unless strengthened. Dr. Marius Barbeau, collecting folksongs of Old France, chose this village as his base of operations.

(370.1) STE. ANNE DES MONTS   This is a pilgrimage spot. Educational institutions here include an agricultural school and a normal school. To the east, Highway No. 6 links up with a road leading to the 2500 square mile Provincial Park high up on the Gaspesian plateau which is open to the public.

The Church of Ste. Anne once prized a relic of their saint, a finger which was lost when the church burned down. Pilgrims, however, still visit the grandiose new church. The distant Shickshock Mountains form the extreme portion of the Appalachian system. One of the longest bridges in Quebec crosses the Ste. Anne River at the west entrance of the village.

(381.6) CAP CHAT (1815)   An outline in rock resembles a cat, but the name of this town is supposed to be a mispronunciation of *Chatte* or *Chastes*, name bestowed by Champlain in honor of a Lieutenant General in the King's service. Egg Island, where Admiral Walker's fleet suffered disaster, is visible in the distance. In 1711, the pilotless fleet crept along in a fog and cracked up with a vengeance on a reef, losing eight ships out of 46 transports, and a thousand men.

(388.7) ST. PAUL DES CAPUCINS   The name comes from rock formations suggesting the silhouettes of Capuchin monks, but only one such shape remains.

(397.4) ST. EDOUARD DES MECHINS   *Méchins* is derived from a mispronunciation of *méchants* (wicked), the name of two capes. Several lakes about eight miles away offer good fishing.

(416.3) STE. FELICITE (1850)   Originally this was known as "Pointe au Massacre," referring to the wreckage of a frigate belonging to the Hovenden-Walker fleet in 1711. By the waterfront is L'Anse au Four (Oven Cove), a cavern shaped

137

Left: Gaspesian express. Right: Man of distinction poses for portrait in fog.

like a huge outdoor oven with a smoke hole at the top — supposed to have been hewn out of the granite by a giant in distant ages. The shore presents "Grosses Roches" (great rocks offshore) and "Anse du Gros Crapaud" (Great Toad Cove); the latter seen in fading light actually looks like a shoreline of "toads."

(424.4) MATANE   The name is taken from the Micmac word for "pool where the beavers fish." Champlain discovered this salmon river which has been open to public fishing, subject, of course, to laws and regulations of the Fish and Game Department. After Gaspé, this is the largest town, an industrial and commercial center. A fine harbor, open even into early winter, with regular steamer service to other ports. Good garages and hotels.

(436.1) ST. ULRIC   Another name for it is Rivière Blanche. Two rivers, one large, one small, are saturated in foam as they course over rock-strewn bottoms. Some of the falls are 100 feet in height, and the power is harnessed to supply several large sawmills. Lakes in the region offer good fishing — deer and small game shooting in the woods, and a fine sandy beach on the shore itself. In the late fall of 1906, a coal-laden ship running too close to shore struck a reef. Nosed toward land, the whole cargo was eventually dumped, a memorable occasion, for at low tide the residents of St. Ulric gathered their full winter's supply of coal.

(445.9) BAIE DES SABLES (Sand Beach)   The bay was originally settled by Scotsmen, but French Canadians gradually took over.

(451.4) METIS SUR MER   Métis means "aspen" or "birch." The second part of the name comes from the bathing beach. Early Scottish colonization, and today a noted English summer resort. Excellent climate. Good fishing, deep sea and fresh water, all sports available.

(466.1) STE. FLAVIE (1829)   Here is the end of Perron Boulevard, named for the Honorable J. L. Perron, Minister of Highways in the twenties.

(475.0)   ST. LUCE   Here is a fine white sand beach. We have the recollection of a local gentleman happily displaying a twenty-pound salmon. An historic mill here was converted into a tourist bureau.

(479.3) POINTE AU PERE   In 1663, this served as a mission post and the name honors the good deeds of Père (Father) Nouvel, a Jesuit. The sanctuary here is dedicated to — you guessed it — Saint Anne. Ocean liners pick up pilots here for the journey up the St. Lawrence.

In 1914, on almost the last day in May, the pilot had just been dropped from the *Empress of Ireland*. The great steamer was breezing along in a light fog, ocean bound, when disaster struck. At 1.55 A.M. she was rammed by the Norwegian collier *Storstad*. The *Empress* sank in fifteen minutes; 1140 lives were lost and but 337 saved. Later the Admiralty Court blamed the Norwegian vessel for changing course just prior to the collision. A monument erected by the railway-steamship system pays respect to the victims, and the unidentified and those unclaimed by relatives are buried nearby in a special cemetery.

(485.4) RIMOUSKI   The town gets its name from the Indian word for "habitation of the dog." The traveler is now approaching the marts of industry: the usual lumber activities, sawmills, factories. The Canadian Postal Service flies the mail of many an ocean liner to Ottawa for national distribution from here. Steamer service at Rimouski plies to important centers of the North Shore region.

(486.9) SACRE COEUR   This agricultural parish was founded in 1875.

(495.6) BIC   The name is a mispronunciation of *Pic* (peak), and was given by Champlain on his earliest Quebec voyage in 1603 to designate the mount dominat-

Fog or fair, the Gaspé North Shore trail runs in and out of bays, under mountains . . . and always at hand the St. Lawrence River.

ing the port. At Massacre Island, off in the bay, once 200 Micmacs attempting to escape to the protection of the Gaspé peninsula region, were ambushed by their arch enemies, the Iroquois, and decimated by tomahawks and arrows as they emerged from a huge cave that had sheltered them for the night.

(505.1) St. Fabien   No comment except that this is a lovely bay and that from 1828 this has been an agricultural site.

(523.4) Trois Pistoles   The name is explained by a hackneyed legend. It seems that in 1621 a French sailor prospecting upriver the source of good drinking water dropped his pewter goblet into the stream by accident. "There go three pistoles!" he cried, referring to the price of the cup.

Trois Pistoles has its own miracle. Nearly a century ago, the men of the village, sensing a quick bonanza, had ventured out on the ice after a herd of seal. Without warning the ice buckled, and the hunters, trapped on a huge ice floe, began to drift toward the open sea. Horror-stricken, the wives and children watched the imminent disaster till they were rallied by the parish priest, and then as a group they began to pray. The great shard of ice suddenly changed its course, began to float back to shore. The story ends happily, for all the men were rescued. Today a monument commemorates the event, as if a town with its own special miracle should ever require a marker to keep the story alive.

(534.8) ILE VERTE (1713) The island owes its name to a description in *Relations des Jésuites* (1663). It is the birthplace of His Eminence Cardinal Rouleau. The kelp industry, along with the usual agricultural activity, has been active here.

(544.9) CACOUNA The Algonquin name stands for "land of the porcupine." The town is agricultural today, but more famous for being a watering place. Many important Canadian and English personages have enjoyed themselves at "Beautiful Cacouna." Bathing, golf, tennis and the like.

(550.9) RIVIERE DU LOUP Here at this busy industrial and commercial city, the tourist must decide whether to cut back into Maine, or to put his car on the steamer ferry which will transport him across the azure St. Lawrence to St. Simeon (for Murray Bay west, or the Saguenay east). In this instance, of course, our itinerary dictates straight on, up the river to Lévis, slightly over 120 miles away.

Rivière du Loup was where Champlain first saw the Loup Indians, called the Wolf tribe. Today it has a population of around ten thousand people. Among other busy activities it is an important railroad center and the site of railroad repair shops.

(557.4) NOTRE DAME DU PORTAGE The second part of the name descends from the military trail built by Governor Haldimand in 1783 to link Rivière du Loup with Halifax. The "portage" thus eliminated a lengthy coastal water journey around the Gaspé.

(566.1) ANDREVILLE This agricultural village was founded in 1791 to honor the first name of an early settler, André Fraser.

(576.9) KAMOURASKA The Indian word means "there are rushes in the water." Old houses and parochial organization dating from 1714.

(582.7) ST. DENIS The place is named in honor of Seigneur Nicolas Juchereau de St. Denis and founded in 1843. From this point it is about one hundred miles to Quebec city.

(589.4) RIVIERE OUELLE Ouelle was a member of Cardinal Richelieu's One Hundred Associates, organized in 1628 for the development of New France. ST. PACOME is just over 100 years old, and is agricultural and industrial. ST. PHILIPPE DE NERI is agricultural. ST. PASCHAL dates from 1827 and is the seat of Kamouraska County. ST. HELENE, 1846, takes pride in its church paintings.

(594.1) STE. ANNE DE LA POCATIERE (1678) Here is one of the leading educational centers in the Province.

(602.1) ST. ROCH DES AULNETS (1734) "Many old houses."

(610.6) ST. JEAN PORT JOLI Founded in 1721, its 1779 church contains the tomb of Philippe Aubert de Gaspé, author of *Anciens Canadiens* and *Memoires*.

140

Products of woodworking and handicrafts are available here. Our constant companion, the St. Lawrence, begins to lose the tincture of salt water and to become solely a fresh-water river.

(619.3) L'ISLET (1679)   Its church dates from 1768; its "Annunciation" is by the first Canadian born painter, the Reverend Aide Créquy.

(626.5) CAP ST. IGNACE   Jesuit missionaries were undoubtedly responsible for its name. The Manoir Gamache here is 250 years old. The Parish Hall, once the Presbytery, dates from 1746.

(633.1) MONTMAGNY (1678)   It was named after Montmagny, the second governor of New France, and in turn was dubbed by the Huron Indians "Ononthio," birthplace of Sir Etienne Paschal Taché, one of the fathers of the celebrated Canadian Confederation. The founder of Joliette, the Honorable Barthélémy Joliette, was born here; thousands of Irish immigrants as well as ministering French-Canadian nuns and priests died here in the typhus epidemic of 1834 to 1838.

(642.5) BERTHIER   The town was named for a captain in the French Carignan Regiment to which the Baron de St. Castin of Castine, Maine, once belonged. Berthier Manor, once the residence of the Seigneur, is 250 years old. Champlain, in 1629, christened the nearby islands "Hunting Islands" — thence the name, Bellechasse County.

(648.3) ST. VALLIER   The second Bishop of Quebec gave his name to this town.

(659.2) BEAUMONT   A lovely church here dates from 1727. Many old houses.

(666.6) LAUZON   The shipbuilding produced here is important throughout the world. Named for the governor of New France who administered the seigniory after 1636. The Bar Harbor-Yarmouth ferry keel was laid here in 1953.

(668.4) LEVIS   Champlain called this tip of land, jutting out into St. Lawrence opposite the Rock of Quebec, Cape Lévy, naming it for Viceroy Henri de Lévis, Duc de Ventadour. Wolfe's guns in 1759 bombarded Quebec from the site of the present-day church Notre Dame de la Victoire. Lévis was the birthplace of his Eminence Cardinal Bégin, a Prince of the Roman Catholic Church. Three ancient English forts are nearby.

(circa 670) QUEBEC   Cartier, we are here! — about 420 years following you and 350 years after Champlain, and almost 200 years behind Wolfe.

Château Frontenac at Quebec — a famous hotel on one of the greatest of rocks, even more celebrated since the historic conferences of World War II. In the foreground is the only statue in the world to both the victor and the vanquished: Wolfe and Montcalm.

XIV

Quebec on the Rock

WHEN OUR UBIQUITOUS EXPLORER, dark-featured, bearded Jacques Cartier, first saw the great rock of Quebec in 1535 from the rail of the *Grande Hermione,* he is supposed to have shouted, *"Quel bec!"* (What a beak!). And at about the same time Cartier also named Canada. Two piloting Indian guides assured him, on reaching the Isle of Orleans, which he called Ile de Bacchus because of its profusion of wild grapes, that he was now in the kingdom of "Canada," in reality a Huron-Iroquois word for "village." A great many years later Charles Dickens was to refer to Quebec as the Gibraltar of America and today, despite a populace no longer clothed in buckles, hoop skirts, jackboots, plumed hats and sabers, its romantic ramparts nonetheless remain, and it is still considered one of the ten best-looking cities in the world.

On his next appearance at Quebec, Cartier met Donnacona, chief of the tribe of the Indian Village Stadacona, which spread across part of the present city limits. In the spring of 1539 Cartier's party, within its moat-encircled little fort below the dark shape of the rock, took stock of its position and found it not good: one of the three ships had been lost and twenty seamen had died of scurvy. It seemed the propitious moment to return to France. Cartier pondered the idea of bringing back some proof of his achievements in the New World. A last dinner party was planned; Donnacona, as guest of honor, attended, and after the repast was shanghaied passively on board the *Grande Hermione.* The scene of poor Donnacona and his ten Indians bidding farewell to their perplexed tribesmen clustered in canoes around Cartier's bark has been a well-worn theme among Canadian painters. Columbus had returned with savages to the court of Spain; Waymouth after his voyage to Camden, Maine, waters in 1605 was to employ the same method.

In France the king received Donnacona with all majesty and various mock honors, conferring on the chief the title of King of Canada. Not one of the touring Indians ever returned.

Cartier sailed back across the ocean on a third trip to Quebec in 1541, but apparently none of the Indians in the reception party asked, at least immediately, "Where's Donnacona?" Doubts as to the welfare of their chief, however, may have permeated eventually, because the next spring the Indians began to be troublesome. Cartier set the jib and made for France on the double.

For the next six decades France, too busy with religious squabbles, gave up all thought of colonization in the New World.

Left: From Dufferin Terrace, Quebec, looking back across the St. Lawrence. Many leagues away is the Gaspé. Right: Champlain's statue at the lower end of the terrace.

Sixty years later Samuel de Champlain, who since 1599 had been far afield visiting Mexico, Louisiana, Mount Desert Island, Castine, Port Royal, Gaspé, and way stations, now put in an appearance. He found no traces of either the village of Stadacona or of Cartier's crude palisade. Champlain, however, built his own stockade, and herewith receives credit for founding Quebec. These were a few frail huts, the "habitation," huddled beneath the cliff. On the lovely Ile d'Orleans, his *habitants* set to work to cultivate its rich soil. This in later years was to produce the most luscious strawberries and little plums, so exquisite in combination with the island's *fromage raffiné,* a distinctive Orleans cheese and a well-guarded family recipe.

As for the Rock, Champlain, who had seen a thing or two, realized that the soaring promontory would be one of the strongholds of the earth, where men could defend a nation. From here he was to pursue far and wide the exploration of New France, country that stretched down the Mississippi to the Gulf. He was to discover Lake Huron and Lake Ontario and of course the lake that bears his name. Thrice the Rock was to be assaulted in Champlain's day, and the last time, when he was too deflated in health to retain it, he was taken to England as prisoner. But when Canada was restored in 1610, Champlain returned as lieutenant-governor of New France, and there he died. His bones are supposedly buried in the city — no one knows where.

At age forty-three in 1610, Champlain had married in France the twelve-year-old Hélène Boullé. But Canada seemed more important than a child bride — Hélène waited ten years before she herself set out for Canada. When her famous husband, who was thirty-one years older, died, Hélène became a nun.

In 1629 the English moved in triumphantly, with Kirke leading the conquest. But Quebec was restored to France by virtue of the Treaty of St. Germain-en-Laye in 1632.

The year 1690 brought Sir William Phips, salvager of buried treasure, High Sheriff, and later Governor of Massachusetts — after a long tour of the Gaspé,

144

where he had been living high off the land. At Quebec, however, he was repulsed by seventy-year-old Louis de Bande, Comte de Frontenac, who, when approached by a blindfolded English envoy with the suggestion that he capitulate, made good his boast that his guns would give the answer to all invaders. Later, according to Bruce Hutchison, in *The Unknown Country,* Frontenac was betrayed by his king and country, even his titled lady remained in France while he existed in Canada. ". . . this gorgeous and fantastic adventurer, who could love, fight, drink, eat, and swagger through battlefields, courts and chateaux of Europe, and through the treacherous forests of Canada! On Frontenac the appreciative modern world has conferred the highest honor. A cigar has been named for him."

The next attempt to reach Quebec came in the form of a great armada under Admiral Hovenden Walker, but nature assisted Quebec by slapping a dire storm against the truculent British fleet which foundered on Egg Island outside Cap Chat.

145

On the other side of the château, the Place d'Armes, calèches, and victorias. The calèche was the first pleasure rig in America.

There was to be no serious threat from the English for almost fifty years. But when it came, in the form of Wolfe's invasion, it was decisive. James Wolfe had been brilliant as a thirty-two-year-old brigadier general at Louisburg under General Jeffrey Amherst the year previously. A slightly built son of a soldier, weak of chin and weak in health from birth, Wolfe found himself a major general at thirty-two, leading 4000 troops against the Citadel, ably supported by the great fleet of Admiral Saunders, all for the greater joy of King George III.

Spectacular seamanship cleared the rapids and reefs of the St. Lawrence, where angels dared not. The amazed Governor Vaudreuil wrote: "The enemy have passed 60 ships of war where we do not risk a vessel 100 tons by night and day."

Meanwhile benign General Joseph de Montcalm-Gozon, victor in four campaigns against the British, checkmated the jockeying tactics of his young adversary on the river below, conscious all the time that the internal situation was not all it should be. "Its stores depleted by crooked politicians," says Bruce Hutchison, "Its walls weakly built by crooked contractors, its money gone to buy silks and perfumes for the French King's mistresses."

"What a country!" writes Montcalm in his dispatch, "Where rogues grow rich and honest men are ruined!"

Weeks and months of despair for Wolfe — occasioned by a disastrous offensive from Montmorency — his broken health is repaired by a meager rest. And now he dares stealthily by night to ascend the heights from Anse au Foulon, today called Wolfe's Cove, a mile and a half from the city. Sentinels are overcome, the summit is gained — to Wolfe's supreme satisfaction, the forces are joined. Wolfe has the advantage in muskets and morale.

Wolfe, had the night before read aloud to his brother officers from Gray's 'Elegy," "The paths of glory lead but to the grave," commented, "Gentlemen, I would rather have written that than beat the French tomorrow!"

Wolfe, member of a family whose generations always died in battle takes a bullet through the wrist. He binds it with a handkerchief. Another smashes his groin; a third bores his shoulder. Told by his surgeon that he cannot live, he murmurs for the history books, "Now God be praised, I die happy." Then one last order from the practical soldier: "Go one of you with all speed to Colonel Burton and tell him to march Webb's regiment down to the St. Charles River, and cut off the retreat of fugitives to the bridge." Meanwhile Montcalm is holding up his end in the field of heroics. Also fatally wounded, he replies: "So much the better, I shall not see the surrender of Quebec." Then he writes a noble letter to Wolfe. In desperation — there is no time for grave digging — a handful of monks and nuns leave his body to the protection of a shell hole in the Ursuline Convent. Four days later Montcalm's forces surrender to the English on the Plains of Abraham. Wolfe's body was transported in the autumn to England.

There was no blood shed at Quebec for fifteen years. The Treaty of Paris in 1763 ceded New France to England; twelve years later England was engaged in a war with her American colonies. The Americans acted on the chance of securing allies among the supposedly smoldering French at Quebec, not so long ago beaten by Wolfe. On November 14, 1775, brilliant, headstrong Benedict Arnold, pet of General Washington — five years before he was to become a traitor and sell out to Clinton — landed a force at the same little cove from which Wolfe had ascended the heights of the Citadel. He was followed the next month by General Mont-

Full circle at Quebec. *Finis.*

gomery, who the year before had already come to Canada, attempting to influence the French to join the Revolution.

Montgomery and 700 men chose a New Year's Eve snowstorm to attack down Champlain Street, just below the Citadel. A blast from a British blockhouse manned by a handful of men — fifty they boast was the number — killed Montgomery and his two aides, Majors Cheseman and McPherson.

As for Arnold, who was supposed to advance along St. Charles Street and join forces with Montgomery at Mountain Hill, he never got there either, having been wounded at the outset. His men pressed on, however, took the first barricade but

147

missed on the next and capitulated. Score: one hundred Americans dead, about five hundred wounded. France had decided to play along with England.

Bunker Hill in the same year (1775) contributed a small souvenir cannon to Quebec. This is shown to Americans with some restrained pride by the guides directing visitors in the Citadel. Though American, it bears no stamp "Made in U.S.A."; there was no U.S.A. when it was cast.

After the conquest of Wolfe nineteenth-century Quebec lost no intensity of color. The incredible Duke of Kent, whom a later Halifax was to know actively, found Quebec just to his liking. Whereas the English had come as conquerors by the sword, the beauties of Quebec were to win the battle of Eros time and time again. Horatio Nelson, who found one of the first of his Lady Hamiltons at Quebec, had to be carried bodily, kicking and struggling in the arms of his shipmates, to the ship's longboat, and out of the embrace of his French Canadian sweetheart.

For a time Quebec, Mother of Canada, lived like a gay Parisienne. Hutchison, who writes so rapturously in his *The Unknown Country,* suggests of this glittering era: " . . . if you could only peer through the keyhole . . . candlelight, hooped skirts, swords, shoe buckles, fans, flirtations and splendid adulteries — as in the Duke of Kent's square, ugly house."

By way of comparison as of today Hutchison takes a gentle poke at Boston. "Probably there is no place in the New World, at least, to which it can be precisely compared. Boston, perhaps, holds as much history. But Boston is an aged spinster, growing fat with good living, virtue triumphant but to love-life unknown. Quebec, though older, is French and, no spinster, has known life, loved it, and relished it all and still looks out with bright knowing eyes from the rock."

Today Quebec is a city of more than 200,000. Ninety per cent of its inhabitants speak French and ninety-seven per cent are Catholic. That Quebec is the largest producer of shoe leather in America is of more importance to the Chamber of Commerce than to this recording of flashback history on wheels. In casual trend we are more concerned in the events that, like the landscape and the edifices, are destined to remain in memory, whether God or man the architect. Industrial accomplishments are all too often ephemeral.

The Quebec city fathers understand the economics of beauty, plus history, and have put teeth in their zoning laws — the like of which is not to be seen in the United States — to protect the past virtues of their fortress city. Upper Town, Lower Town; Sous-le-Cap, the narrowest street in North America; and still piercing the fortifications, the ancient gates of St. Louis, Kent, and St. Jean, Notre Dame des Victoires, where once was celebrated the successful repulse of Hovenden Walker, and Phips; above the post office the ancient stone of the golden dog (le Chien d'Or) the old market, the Victorian parliament buildings, and Sailors Town, which has played a part in more than one Hollywood production; add to this list l'Université de Laval, the premier French-Canadian ecclesiastical university, les Ramparts, with some of the old cannon still on guard, le Couvent des Ursulines, with its memories of Montcalm and a sanctuary lamp that has burned since 1717, l'Hôtel Dieu, l'Hôpital Général, St. Martins-in-the-Fields, Trafalgar Square — these are the things that make Quebec.

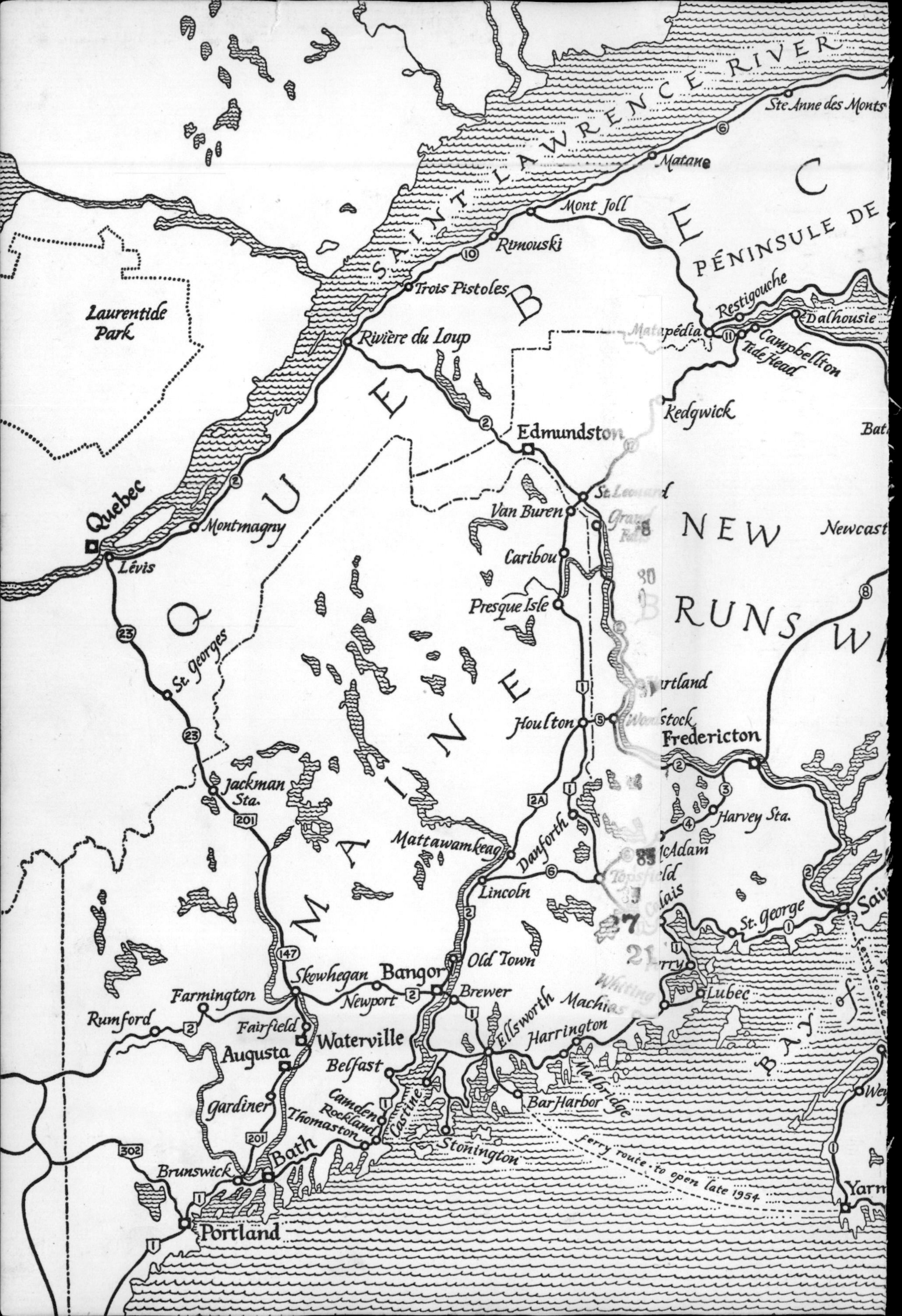

SAINT LAWRENCE RIVER

Ste Anne des Monts

Matane

Mont Joli

Rimouski

Trois Pistoles

Laurentide Park

Rivière du Loup

PÉNINSULE DE

Restigouche

Dalhousie

Matapédia

Campbellton

Tide Head

Kedgwick

Bath

Quebec

Montmagny

Lévis

St. Georges

Edmundston

St. Leonard

Van Buren

Grand Falls

Caribou

NEW

Newcast

Presque Isle

BRUNS

WI

Jackman Sta.

201

Houlton

Woodstock

Fredericton

Portland

80

Harvey Sta.

McAdam

Topsfield

St. George

Sai

Mattawamkeag

Danforth

Lincoln

Calais

Old Town

Whiting

rry

Lubec

Skowhegan

Bangor

Brewer

Ellsworth

Machias

Harrington

Farmington

Newport

Rumford

Fairfield

Augusta

Waterville

Belfast

Milbridge

Bar Harbor

Wey

Gardiner

Camden

Rockland

Castine

Stonington

ferry route to open late 1954

Bath

Thomaston

Brunswick

Portland

Yarm

MAINE

QUEBEC

BAY